T1-BKE-762

DICKINSON PUBLIC LIBRARY

D0468205

Addiction

David Haugen and Susan Musser, *Book Editors*

GREENHAVEN PRESS
A part of Gale, Cengage Learning

Detroit • New York • San Francisco • New Haven, Conn • Waterville, Maine • London

Elizabeth Des Chenes, *Director, Publishing Solutions*

For more information, contact:
Greenhaven Press
27500 Drake Rd.
Farmington Hills, MI 48331-3535
Or you can visit our Internet site at gale.cengage.com

Articles in Greenhaven Press anthologies are often edited for length to meet page requirements. In addition, original titles of these works are changed to clearly present the main thesis and to explicitly indicate the author's opinion. Every effort is made to ensure that Greenhaven Press accurately reflects the original intent of the authors. Every effort has been made to trace the owners of copyrighted material.

LIBRARY OF CONGRESS CATALOGING-IN-PUBLICATION DATA

Addiction / David Haugen and Susan Musser, book editors.
p. cm. -- (Introducing issues with opposing viewpoints)
Includes bibliographical references and index.
ISBN 978-0-7377-4164-3 (hbk.)
1. Substance abuse. 2. Substance abuse--United States. 3. Substance abuse--Treatment. I. Haugen, David M., 1969- II. Musser, Susan.
HV4998.A3185 2013
362.29--dc23

2012041151

Printed in the United States of America
1 2 3 4 5 6 7 17 16 15 14 13

Contents

Chapter 3: What Policies Can Reduce Addiction?

Foreword

Indulging in a wide spectrum of ideas, beliefs, and perspectives is a critical cornerstone of democracy. After all, it is often debates over differences of opinion, such as whether to legalize abortion, how to treat prisoners, or when to enact the death penalty, that shape our society and drive it forward. Such diversity of thought is frequently regarded as the hallmark of a healthy and civilized culture. As the Reverend Clifford Schutjer of the First Congregational Church in Mansfield, Ohio, declared in a 2001 sermon, "Surrounding oneself with only like-minded people, restricting what we listen to or read only to what we find agreeable is irresponsible. Refusing to entertain doubts once we make up our minds is a subtle but deadly form of arrogance." With this advice in mind, Introducing Issues with Opposing Viewpoints books aim to open readers' minds to the critically divergent views that comprise our world's most important debates.

Introducing Issues with Opposing Viewpoints simplifies for students the enormous and often overwhelming mass of material now available via print and electronic media. Collected in every volume is an array of opinions that captures the essence of a particular controversy or topic. Introducing Issues with Opposing Viewpoints books embody the spirit of nineteenth-century journalist Charles A. Dana's axiom: "Fight for your opinions, but do not believe that they contain the whole truth, or the only truth." Absorbing such contrasting opinions teaches students to analyze the strength of an argument and compare it to its opposition. From this process readers can inform and strengthen their own opinions, or be exposed to new information that will change their minds. Introducing Issues with Opposing Viewpoints is a mosaic of different voices. The authors are statesmen, pundits, academics, journalists, corporations, and ordinary people who have felt compelled to share their experiences and ideas in a public forum. Their words have been collected from newspapers, journals, books, speeches, interviews, and the Internet, the fastest growing body of opinionated material in the world.

Introducing Issues with Opposing Viewpoints shares many of the well-known features of its critically acclaimed parent series, Opposing Viewpoints. The articles are presented in a pro/con format, allowing readers to absorb divergent perspectives side by side. Active reading questions preface each viewpoint, requiring the student to approach the material thoughtfully and carefully. Useful charts, graphs, and cartoons supplement each article. A thorough introduction provides readers with crucial background on an issue. An annotated bibliography points the reader toward articles, books, and websites that contain additional information on the topic. An appendix of organizations to contact contains a wide variety of charities, nonprofit organizations, political groups, and private enterprises that each hold a position on the issue at hand. Finally, a comprehensive index allows readers to locate content quickly and efficiently.

Introducing Issues with Opposing Viewpoints is also significantly different from Opposing Viewpoints. As the series title implies, its presentation will help introduce students to the concept of opposing viewpoints and learn to use this material to aid in critical writing and debate. The series' four-color, accessible format makes the books attractive and inviting to readers of all levels. In addition, each viewpoint has been carefully edited to maximize a reader's understanding of the content. Short but thorough viewpoints capture the essence of an argument. A substantial, thought-provoking essay question placed at the end of each viewpoint asks the student to further investigate the issues raised in the viewpoint, compare and contrast two authors' arguments, or consider how one might go about forming an opinion on the topic at hand. Each viewpoint contains sidebars that include at-a-glance information and handy statistics. A Facts About section located in the back of the book further supplies students with relevant facts and figures.

Following in the tradition of the Opposing Viewpoints series, Greenhaven Press continues to provide readers with invaluable exposure to the controversial issues that shape our world. As John Stuart Mill once wrote: "The only way in which a human being can make some approach to knowing the whole of a subject is by hearing what can be said about it by persons of every variety of opinion and studying all modes in which it can be looked at by every character of mind. No wise man ever acquired his wisdom in any mode but this." It is to this principle that Introducing Issues with Opposing Viewpoints books are dedicated.

Introduction

According to the 2010 National Survey on Drug Use and Health of the US Department of Health and Human Services, alcohol and drug addictions are still significant national concerns. As the survey reported, 2 million Americans aged twelve to twenty admitted to being heavy consumers of alcohol, and 6.5 million classified themselves as binge drinkers. In addition, 22.6 million Americans over twelve years of age listed themselves as current or former users of illicit drugs. The survey also found that over 6 million children live with a parent who has a drug addiction. While some statistics—such as the number of young drug users—show a decline over the past two decades, other trends are on the rise. For example, since 1990, the Department of Health and Human Services estimates that the number of individuals who take prescription drugs illegally has increased by over 500 percent and that the number of deaths related to drug overdoses has risen by more than 540 percent since 1980. In his introduction to the 2012 National Drug Control Strategy, President Barack Obama affirmed, "Our Nation still faces serious drug-related challenges. . . . We must ensure continued support for policies and programs that reduce drug use and its enormous costs to American society."

According to R. Gil Kerlikowske, the director of the White House Office of National Drug Control Policy, the administration's drug control strategy defines drug addiction as a public health issue. This assessment, according to Kerlikowske, is based on the concept that addiction is a chronic disease of the brain that can be cured with treatment. In an April 18, 2012, viewpoint for the *Huffington Post*, Kerlikowske stated, "Our emphasis on addressing the drug problem through a public health approach is grounded in decades of research and scientific study. There is overwhelming evidence that drug prevention and treatment programs achieve meaningful results with significant long-term cost savings." Indeed, the Obama strategy allocates more money to drug treatment programs than that doled out under his predecessor, George W. Bush, and Obama hopes that if Congress and the courts permit the full implementation of the 2010 Patient Protections and Affordable Care Act, then health insurers will be compelled to pay for drug treatment programs as part of comprehensive coverage. The administration touts this approach as a socially and fiscally better alternative to inflating the costly burden of domestic drug enforcement and incarceration.

Some observers are not pleased with the strategy's downplaying of enforcement, while those at the opposite end of the policy spectrum may criticize the president's plan for not simply legalizing drugs and ending the $20 billion to $25 billion per year spent on prohibition. On May 8, 2012, John Walsh, senior associate of the Washington Office on Latin America, gave a very detailed review of the 2012 strategy. Walsh claims the administration's policy may disparage the enforcement and incarceration approach as costly and ineffective, but the budget for these elements is still comparable to their counterparts under the George W. Bush policy. The difference, Walsh asserts, is that "federal treatment spending during the Obama administration has already been measurably higher than during the Bush administration." As Walsh concludes, "The Obama administration deserves credit for at least acknowledging the wasteful excesses of domestic drug enforcement and for taking steps to bolster treatment. But talk of a revolution in U.S. drug policy is still premature."

Treating addiction as a health issue, however, is still a controversial approach. Forcing insurers to cover an addiction to an illegal substance, for example, is not without its detractors, and designating addiction as a brain illness has not met with approval in all scientific quarters. On June 16, 2011, addiction expert Stanton Peele wrote a piece for the *Huffington Post* in which he analyzed current thought on the illness model. Citing various theories on how the brain responds to drugs, Peele pointed out what he sees as three problems in the assumption that changes in brain chemistry result in addiction. First, he states that all drugs act differently on the brain, affecting the release of the pleasure-inducing neurochemical dopamine in a variety of ways. Second, Peele notes that it is difficult to account for other addictions—such as video game addiction or compulsive gambling—under the same umbrella as drug addiction because brain reaction in these cases may be quite different. Finally, he contends that not everyone who experiments with an addictive substance becomes addicted. Peele writes, "In fact, no neurochemical or brain differences have ever been found between addicts and others *prior to taking drugs*. . . . That there is something inherent in the person to be found there—in mental illness and addiction—is received wisdom, not empirical fact."

Also, many argue that portraying addiction as a brain disease opens the door to defining all excessive behaviors as medical illnesses. Those who believe the government is already too involved in the personal habits of individuals condemn the notion that insurance companies might one day be paying the treatment costs of a shopaholic or a cell phone addict. In a 2006 article for the *Chicago Sun-Times*, Morris E. Chafetz, the founder of the National Institute on Alcohol Abuse and Alcoholism, makes the argument that defining compulsive behaviors as mental disorders absolves individuals of the personal responsibility to rein in their bad behaviors. *Introducing Issues with Opposing Viewpoints: Addiction* brings together views from an array of commentators to offer a varied picture of addiction—its causes and treatments—in America. Some of the assembled experts focus on how addiction should be modeled; others debate the successes and failures of treatments and the public policies that support them. Together, the viewpoints in this anthology address the "drug-related challenges" President Obama spoke of in the National Drug Control Strategy as the ethical and policy-related choices the country faces as it continues to fight to control the problems of addiction.

Chapter 1

How Should Addiction Be Defined and Treated?

A girl searches for a gambling website, credit card in hand. Whether gambling or other behaviors are true addictions is hotly debated.

Addiction Is a Medical Phenomenon

Jennifer Matesa and Jed Bickman

In the following viewpoint Jennifer Matesa and Jed Bickman report that new evidence from the American Society of Addiction Medicine (ASAM) shows that addictive behavior is a medical illness and not simply a mental disorder. As the authors state, this conclusion emphasizes that individuals succumb to addictive behaviors due to abnormal wiring that affects the reward processes of the brain. They note that ASAM researchers do not discount the impact of treatments that seek to address more than biological issues, but these experts maintain that the biological aspects cannot be ignored. According to Metesa and Bickman, this conclusion has far-reaching consequences—from correcting the widespread notion that addicts suffer from a moral failure to contemplating how the new definition will affect insurance and treatment coverage. Matesa is an author who writes about addiction issues on her blog, *Guinevere Gets Sober*. Bickman is a writer whose pieces have appeared in the *Nation*, the *Huffington Post*, and other outlets.

"Addiction [is] a full-bore biological illness."

Jennifer Matesa and Jed Bickman, "A New View of Addiction Stirs Up a Scientific Storm," *The Fix*, August 16, 2011. www.thefix.com.

AS YOU READ, CONSIDER THE FOLLOWING QUESTIONS:

1. How do the ASAM and DSM differ in their definition of addiction, according to Matesa and Bickman?
2. As the authors explain, what parts of the neurological pathways are compromised by the abnormalities that predispose individuals toward addiction?
3. As the authors mention, why do physicians like Neil Capretto believe it is important to bring addiction "into the scope of other diseases"?

If you think addiction is all about booze, drugs, sex, gambling, food and other irresistible vices, think again. And if you believe that a person has a choice whether or not to indulge in an addictive behavior, get over it. The American Society of Addiction Medicine (ASAM) blew the whistle on these deeply held notions with its official release of a new document defining addiction as a chronic neurological disorder involving many brain functions, most notably a devastating imbalance in the so-called reward circuitry. This fundamental impairment in the experience of pleasure literally compels the addict to chase the chemical highs produced by substances like drugs and alcohol and obsessive behaviors like sex, food and gambling.

Addiction Is an Illness

The definition, a result of a four-year process involving more than 80 leading experts in addiction and neurology, emphasizes that addiction is a primary illness—in other words, it's not caused by mental health issues such as mood or personality disorders, putting to rest the popular notion that addictive behaviors are a form of "self-medication" to, say, ease the pain of depression or anxiety.

Indeed, the new neurologically focused definition debunks, in whole or in part, a host of common conceptions about addiction. Addiction, the statement declares, is a "bio-psycho-socio-spiritual" illness characterized by (a) damaged decision-making (affecting learning, perception, and judgment) and by (b) persistent risk and/or recurrence of relapse; the unambiguous implications are that (a) addicts have no control over their addictive behaviors and (b) total abstinence is, for some addicts, an unrealistic goal of effective treatment.

The bad behaviors themselves are all symptoms of addiction, not the disease itself. "The state of addiction is not the same as the state of intoxication," the ASAM takes pains to point out. Far from being evidence of a failure of will or morality, the behaviors are the addict's attempt to resolve the general "dysfunctional emotional state" that develops in tandem with the disease. In other words, conscious choice plays little or no role in the actual state of addiction; as a result, a *person cannot choose not to be addicted.* The most an addict can do is *choose not to use* the substance or engage in the behavior that reinforces the entire self-destructive reward-circuitry loop.

Viewing All Addictions as One Disease

Yet ASAM pulls no punches when it comes to the negative consequences of addiction, declaring it an illness that "can cause disability or premature death, especially when left untreated or treated inadequately."

The new definition leaves no doubt that all addictions—whether to alcohol, heroin or sex, say—are fundamentally the same. Dr. Raju Haleja, former president of the Canadian Society for Addiction Medicine and the chair of the ASAM committee that crafted the new definition, told *The Fix,* "We are looking at addiction as one disease, as opposed to those who see them as separate diseases. Addiction is addiction. It doesn't matter what cranks your brain in that direction, once it has changed direction, you're vulnerable to all addiction." That the society has stamped a diagnosis of sex or gambling or food addiction as every bit as medically valid as addiction to alcohol or heroin or crystal meth may spark more controversy than its subtler but equally far-reaching assertions.

The new definition comes as the American Psychiatric Association (APA) is undertaking a highly publicized, decade-in-the-making revision of its own definition of addiction in its *Diagnostic and Statistical Manual of Mental Disorders* [DSM]—the bible of the mental health profession. The APA's DSM will have a larger effect on public health policies that guide addiction treatment, largely because insurance companies are mandated by law to use the DSM diagnostic categories and criteria to decide which treatments they will pay for.

A girl prepares heroin for injection. Many scientists are coming to believe that addiction is a neurological disorder involving many brain functions, and what the person is addicted to is irrelevant.

Dr. Haleja told *The Fix* that the ASAM definition arose partly out of a disagreement with the DSM committee; although the DSM will define addiction as a disease, its symptoms (and therefore diagnostic criteria) will still be viewed mostly as discrete behaviors. Also, the DSM will define each type of addiction as a separate disease, instead of the singular and unified notion of disease that the ASAM proposes. "In terms of treatment, it becomes very important that people don't focus on one aspect of the disease, but the disease as a whole," says Haleja. . . .

The New Addiction Model's Impact on Treatment

Though addicts can't choose not to be addicts, they can choose to get treatment. Recovery, ASAM says, is best realized not just by self-management and mutual support groups such as 12-step fellowships, but also with trained professional help.

Some addiction-medicine specialists see the sweeping new definition as a validation of what has, since the publication of *Alcoholics*

Anonymous in 1939, come to be known as "the disease concept" of addiction. "Many people in the population at large see addiction as a moral problem—'Why don't they just stop?'" says Dr. Neil Capretto, medical director of Gateway Rehabilitation Center in Pittsburgh and an active ASAM member. "For experienced people working in addiction medicine for years, we know it's a brain disease."

Does this statement push the 12 steps, the mainstay of many treatment centers, programs and clinicians, toward obsolescence? After all, when a problem is declared to be a "medical" issue, doesn't that imply that the solution should also be "medical"—as in doctors and drugs? "Both approaches have applicability," says Dr. Marc Galanter, professor of psychiatry at New York University, founding director of its Division of Alcohol and Substance Abuse as well as director of its Fellowship Training Program in Addiction Psychiatry. "The fact that addiction is a disease doesn't mean it's *only* susceptible to drugs." Says Capretto: "This new definition does not say that psychological or spiritual approaches are not important. My concern is that some people who really don't understand the broader scope of addiction will see it only as a disease of brain cells. We're not treating computers—it's in the total human being who is, as the definition says, a 'bio-psycho-socio-spiritual' creature, and who will still need help in those areas."

Fast Fact

A March 2011 publication by the National Institute on Drug Abuse states that people addicted to drugs are twice as likely as the general population to be diagnosed with mood and anxiety disorders.

A Predisposition to Addictive Behavior

With its no-stone-unturned statement (it runs to eight pages, single-spaced, including footnotes), ASAM has come down—mostly—on one side of the chicken-and-egg question that has long befuddled people interested in addiction, physicians and recovering addicts alike: which came first, the neurological disorder or the compulsive behaviors and substance use? The definition states that abnormalities in the neurological system's reward wiring—communication between areas of the brain, particularly those that process memory, emotional response and pleasure—come first, and drive the addict into a doomed pursuit to compensate for the reward-system imbalance through the addictive behavior. But later, the document notes that these behaviors themselves can damage the reward circuitry and lead to impaired impulse control and addiction.

The statement conforms, in its general outlines, with the prevailing premise in cutting-edge addiction science that the natural reward system designed to support human survival becomes overtaken or highjacked by the chemical payoff provided by substance use or addictive behaviors. "The reward circuitry bookmarks things that are important: eating food, nurturing children, having sex, sustaining intimate friendships," says Dr. Mark Publicker, medical director of Mercy Recovery Center in Portland—Maine's largest rehab—and former Regional Chief of Addiction Medicine for Kaiser Permanente Mid-Atlantic Region.

When we use alcohol or drugs, Publicker says, the chemical reward—the "high"—is many times more powerful than the natural circuitry's reward, and the neurological system adapts to the flood of neurotransmitters. "But because we didn't evolve as a species with OxyContin or crack cocaine, that adaptive mechanism overshoots. So it becomes impossible to experience a normal sense of pleasure," he continues. "Use of the substance then happens at the expense of what otherwise would promote survival. If you think about it from that standpoint, it begins to account for illness and premature death." An active addict has a very high risk of early death via sickness or suicide.

Factors That Influence Addiction

The statement raises repeated alarms about the danger posed by the development by teens and young adults of habits of consumption of substances because their brains are still in the process of maturation, and the chemical "hijacking" of the reward system may result in earlier and more serious addiction behaviors. While firmly grounded in the neurological disease model of addiction, the definition by no means discounts genes (it attributes about half of the cause to your DNA inheritance). It's careful to say that environmental factors affect whether and how much the genetics will tip the scales. The statement notes that "resiliencies" acquired through parenting and life

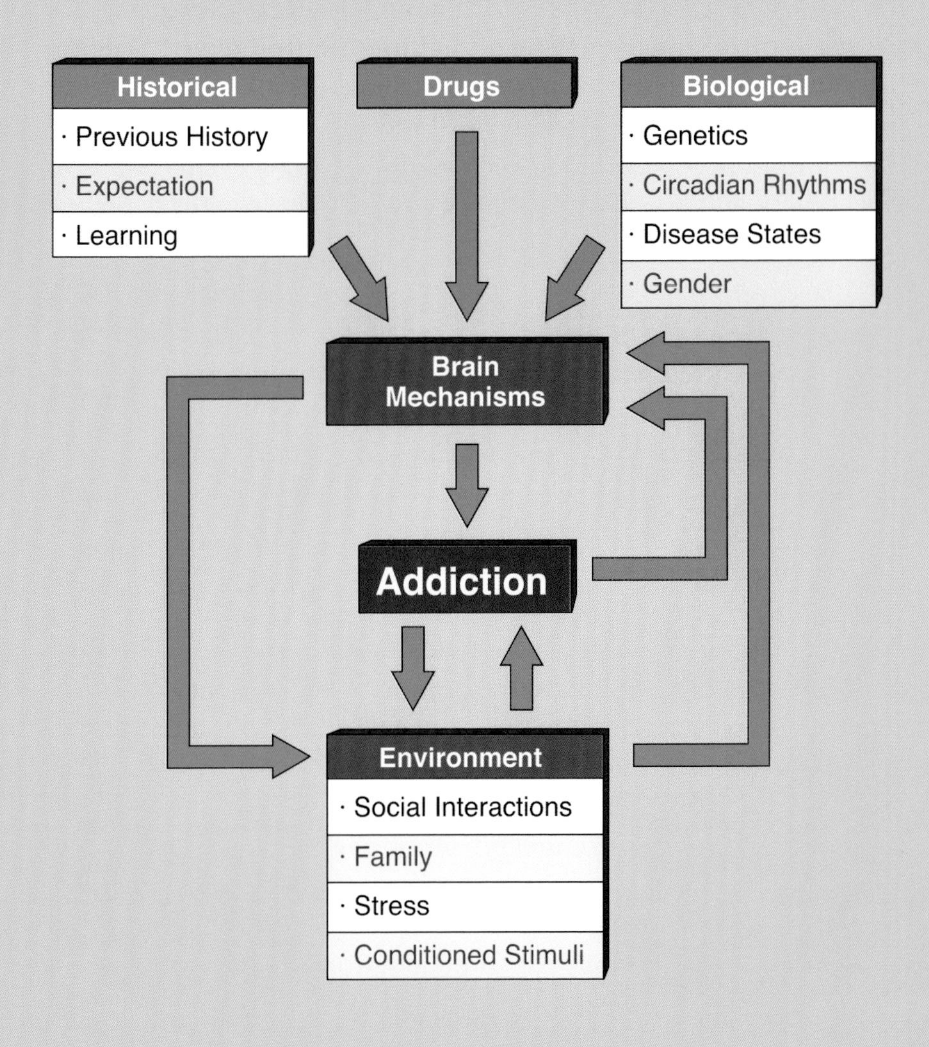

Taken from: National Institute on Drug Abuse. "Addiction Is a Chronic Disease," n.d. http://archives.drugabuse.gov.

experience can inhibit genetic expression of addiction. "Genetics is tendency, not destiny," Capretto says.

Psychological and environmental factors, such as exposure to trauma or overwhelming stress, distorted ideas about life's meaning, a damaged sense of self, and breakdown in connections with others and with "the transcendent (referred to as God by many, the Higher

Power by 12-steps groups, or higher consciousness by others)" are also acknowledged as having an influence.

In addition, ASAM further says that understanding reward systems is just a part of understanding addiction's neurobiology. Scientists are still trying to comprehend how some addicts become preoccupied with certain drugs or behaviors and other addicts with others; how some addicts become triggered to use by some events that don't affect others; and how cravings can persist for decades after a complete recovery.

Treating Behaviors and Biology

The statement attempts to put forth diagnostic hallmarks, all of which are behavioral: inability to abstain; impaired impulse control; cravings; diminished grasp of one's problems; and problematic emotional responses.

Is it a problem that the definition is incapable of pointing to a quantifiable diagnostic marker of this illness? "I may be stating the obvious, here," Publicker says, sighing, "but you don't need to do brain imaging to identify an active alcoholic."

In fact it emphasizes that "the quantity and frequency" of addictive symptoms—like how many drinks you down in a day or how many hours you spend masturbating—is no more or less of a marker than the "qualitative [and] pathological way" the addict responds to stressors and cues by continued pursuit in the face of growing adverse consequences.

Publicker, an active ASAM member for 30 years and a proponent of medication-assisted therapy for addiction, notes that addiction recovery depends on treatment of psychological, social and spiritual aspects of the illness—not just its biological aspects. "It's called medication-assisted therapy, not therapy-assisted medication," he says. "Medication alone fails. I've seen this over a very long career. But it can really make a difference in people struggling to relapse."

He draws the analogy with depression: "If you ask most people what depression is, they'll answer it's a serotonin deficiency disorder and that the solution is to put somebody on an SSRI [selective serotonin reuptake inhibitor]. But that's a simplistic and inefficient way of managing depression. Medication can be helpful, but it needs to be combined with talk. We live in an era now where talk is not reimbursed. "It remains to be seen whether ASAM's new branding of addiction as a full-bore biological illness will help addicts obtain reimbursement for treatment. In terms of insurers, clarifying that the illness has "biological roots"—stipulating that it's not the patient's fault he or she has the illness—may break down reimbursement roadblocks.

Capretto agrees: "Things like this definition help bring addiction more into the scope of other diseases, so for the future it will mean fewer barriers for people wanting to get help."

One of ASAM's unstated goals was obviously to fight against the stubborn social stigma against addiction experienced by many addicts. "There's no question they set out to de-stigmatize addiction," Publicker says. "Nobody chooses to be an addict. The concern that I have is placing blame on the patient. It takes a very long time for the brain to normalize. While it's waiting to happen, you're feeling bad, your thinking is impaired, and it's a setup for relapse. Patients are likely to be blamed for relapse, and families see them as unmotivated and weak. But that's the disease of addiction."

EVALUATING THE AUTHOR'S ARGUMENTS:

The authors of this viewpoint contend that one of the goals of the ASAM report was to "fight against the stubborn social stigma against addiction experienced by many addicts." Does this observation change the way in which you view the claims made in the viewpoint? Explain why or why not.

The Surprising Truth About Addiction

Stanton Peele

Stanton Peele is a licensed psychologist who frequently writes for *Psychology Today*. In the following viewpoint Peele argues that more people quit addictions than submit to and maintain them and do so on their own without therapy. He contends that it is ridiculous to exempt addiction from our typical beliefs about change. If a person can change their short temper, then why not their addiction? Peele claims that the majority of those who have quit addiction to tobacco, heroin, cocaine, and alcohol have done so on their own. He believes that the fact is that change is the same in all areas of life—even addiction. If an individual wants it badly enough he or she can and will change.

"More people overcome addictions than do not."

AS YOU READ, CONSIDER THE FOLLOWING QUESTIONS:

1. As stated by Peele, what is "at the top of the charts in terms of difficulty of quitting"?
2. According to the viewpoint, what happened in 1992 regarding addiction treatment?
3. As stated in the article, what is the second most effective approach to overcoming addiction?

Stanton Peele, "The Surprising Truth About Addiction," *Psychology Today,* May 1, 2004.

More people quit addictions than maintain them, and they do so on their own. That's not to say it happens overnight. People succeed when they recognize that the addiction interferes with something they value—and when they develop the confidence that they can change.

Change is natural. You no doubt act very differently in many areas of your life now compared with how you did when you were a teenager. Likewise, over time you will probably overcome or ameliorate certain behaviors: a short temper, crippling insecurity.

For some reason, we exempt addiction from our beliefs about change. In both popular and scientific models, addiction is seen as locking you into an inescapable pattern of behavior. Both folk wisdom, as represented by Alcoholics Anonymous, and modern neuroscience regard addiction as a virtually permanent brain disease. No matter how many years ago your uncle Joe had his last drink, he is still considered an alcoholic. The very word addict confers an identity that admits no other possibilities. It incorporates the assumption that you can't, or won't, change.

But this fatalistic thinking about addiction doesn't jibe with the facts. More people overcome addictions than do not. And the vast majority do so without therapy. Quitting may take several tries, and people may not stop smoking, drinking or using drugs altogether. But eventually they succeed in shaking dependence.

Kicking these habits constitutes a dramatic change, but the change need not occur in a dramatic way. So when it comes to addiction treatment, the most effective approaches rely on the counterintuitive principle that less is often more. Successful treatment places the responsibility for change squarely on the individual and acknowledges that positive events in other realms may jump-start change.

Consider the experience of American soldiers returning from the war in Vietnam, where heroin use and addiction was widespread. In 90 percent of cases, when GIs left the pressure cooker of the battle zone, they also shed their addictions—in vivo proof that drug addiction can be just a matter of where in life you are.

Of course, it took more than a plane trip back from Asia for these men to overcome drug addiction. Most soldiers experienced dramatically altered lives when they returned. They left the anxiety, fear and boredom of the war arena and settled back into their home environ-

"Have a cigar. Go ahead—they're bubblegum," cartoon by Bill Abbott, www.CartoonStock.com. Copyright © by Bill Abbott. Reproduction rights obtainable from www.CartoonStock.com. Reproduced by permission.

ments. They returned to their families, formed new relationships, developed work skills.

Smoking is at the top of the charts in terms of difficulty of quitting. But the majority of ex-smokers quit without any aid—neither nicotine patches nor gum, Smokenders groups nor hypnotism. (Don't take my word for it; at your next social gathering, ask how many people have quit smoking on their own.) In fact, as many cigarette smokers quit on their own, an even higher percentage of heroin and cocaine addicts and alcoholics quit without treatment. It is simply more difficult to keep these habits going through adulthood. It's hard to go to Disney World with your family while you are shooting heroin. Addicts who quit on their own typically report that they did so in order to achieve normalcy.

Every year, the National Survey on Drug Use and Health interviews Americans about their drug and alcohol habits. Ages 18 to 25 constitute the peak period of drug and alcohol use. In 2002, the latest year for which data are available, 22 percent of Americans between ages 18 and 25 were abusing or were dependent on a substance, versus only 3 percent of those aged 55 to 59. These data show that most people overcome their substance abuse, even though most of them do not enter treatment.

How do we know that the majority aren't seeking treatment? In 1992, the National Institute on Alcohol Abuse and Alcoholism conducted one of the largest surveys of substance use ever, sending Census Bureau workers to interview more than 42,000 Americans about their lifetime drug and alcohol use. Of the 4,500-plus respondents who had ever been dependent on alcohol, only 27 percent had gone to treatment of any kind, including Alcoholics Anonymous. In this group, one-third were still abusing alcohol.

Fast Fact

The Federal Bureau of Prisons reports that as of July 28, 2012, federal inmates incarcerated for drug offenses accounted for 47.9 percent of the total inmate population.

Of those who never had any treatment, only about one-quarter were currently diagnosable as alcohol abusers. This study, known as the National Longitudinal Alcohol Epidemiologic Survey, indicates first that treatment is not a cure-all, and second that it is not necessary. The vast majority of Americans who were alcohol dependent, about three-quarters, never underwent treatment. And fewer of them were abusing alcohol than were those who were treated.

This is not to say that treatment can't be useful. But the most successful treatments are nonconfrontational approaches that allow self-propelled change. Psychologists at the University of New Mexico led by William Miller tabulated every controlled study of alcoholism treatment they could find. They concluded that the leading therapy was barely a therapy at all but a quick encounter between patient and health-care worker in an ordinary medical setting. The intervention is sometimes as brief as a doctor looking at the results of liver-function tests and telling a patient to cut down on his drinking. Many patients then decide to cut back—and do!

As brief interventions have evolved, they have become more structured. A physician may simply review the amount the patient drinks, or use a checklist to evaluate the extent of a drinking problem. The doctor then typically recommends and seeks agreement from the patient on a goal (usually reduced drinking rather than complete abstinence). More severe alcoholics would typically be referred out for specialized treatment. A range of options is discussed (such as attending AA, engaging in activities incompatible with drinking or using a self-help manual). A spouse or family member might be involved in the planning. The patient is then scheduled for a future visit, where progress can be checked. A case monitor might call every few weeks to see whether the person has any questions or problems.

The second most effective approach is motivational enhancement, also called motivational interviewing. This technique throws the deci-

According to the author, having an addiction such as smoking does not mean a person cannot change, because more people overcome addictions than those who do not, usually without therapy.

The Price of Selected Addiction Rehabilitation Centers

Substance Abuse Center	Price
Cliffside Malibu	$53,000/month
Betty Ford Center	$32,000/month
Hanley Center	$24,600/month
Hazelden	$28,300/month
Treatment Center	$21,000/month
Pride Institute	$19,600/month
Back to Basics Outdoor Adventures	$7,500/month
Cri-Help	$6,000/month

Taken from: *The Fix*. "Rehab Reviews," 2011. www.thefix.com. Compiled and edited from site.

sion to quit or reduce drinking—and to find the best methods for doing so—back on the individual. In this case, the therapist asks targeted questions that prompt the individual to reflect on his drinking in terms of his own values and goals. When patients resist, the therapist does not argue with the individual but explores the person's ambivalence about change so as to allow him or her to draw his own conclusions: "You say that you like to be in control of your behavior, yet you feel when you drink you are often not in charge. Could you just clarify that for me?"

Miller's team found that the list of most effective treatments for alcoholism included a few more surprises. Self-help manuals were highly successful. So was the community-reinforcement approach, which addresses the person's capacity to deal with life, notably marital relationships, work issues (such as simply getting a job), leisure planning and social-group formation (a buddy might be provided, as in AA, as a resource to encourage sobriety). The focus is on developing life skills, such as resisting pressures to drink, coping with stress (at work and in relationships) and building communication skills.

These findings square with what we know about change in other areas of life: People change when they want it badly enough and when they feel strong enough to face the challenge, not when they're humiliated or coerced. An approach that empowers and offers positive reinforcement is preferable to one that strips the individual of agency. These techniques are most likely to elicit real changes, however short of perfect and hard-won they may be.

EVALUATING THE AUTHOR'S ARGUMENTS:

Stanton Peele asserts that addicts have the ability to quit and inspire change—they just have to want it badly enough. Do you agree with Peele's assessment? Explain why or why not.

Quest for Vaccines to Treat Addiction

"'These vaccines have the potential to transform the way we treat drug addiction.'"

Mark Long

In the following viewpoint Mark Long, a reporter for the *Wall Street Journal,* reveals how scientists are working on vaccines to help addicts kick drug habits. Long explains that the vaccines trigger the body's immune system to stop the chemicals in the drugs from reaching the brain and arrest the normal feelings of pleasure. Current vaccines have focused on nicotine addiction and have had mixed results, Long writes, but researchers are still hopeful that small successes will point the way toward better outcomes as the vaccines are improved.

AS YOU READ, CONSIDER THE FOLLOWING QUESTIONS:

1. Why does the immune system not naturally respond to addictive drugs in the body, according to Long?
2. As the author relates, out of every three smokers who try to quit smoking each year, how many are typically successful?
3. In the vaccine's Phase II trials as reported by Long, how many times more likely were smokers taking NicVAX to be off cigarettes forty-four weeks after vaccination than were control subjects?

Mark Long, "Quest for Vaccines to Treat Addiction," *Wall Street Journal,* vol. 257, no. 102, May 3, 2011, pp. D1–D2.

Frustrated by the high relapse rate of traditional addiction treatments, scientists are working on a strategy that recruits the body's own defenses to help addicts kick drug habits.

The new approach uses injected vaccines to block some addictive substances from reaching the brain. If a vaccinated addict on the path to recovery slips and indulges in a drug, such as tobacco or cocaine, no pleasure will result.

"You still have to mentally say to yourself, 'I'm not going to do this,' but it's so much easier to say it when you know if you light a cigarette, you're not going to get any pleasure out of it," says Stephen Ballou, a 56-year-old banker who got a nicotine vaccine in a 2007 clinical trial to help kick his pack-a-day habit. He says he hasn't smoked since.

Some medications currently available to treat addictions typically work by mimicking a drug in the brain. For example, methadone stands in for heroin and the nicotine patch for cigarettes. Other medications block activity in the brain's reward system. Alkermes Inc.'s once-monthly Vivitrol injection does this for alcoholics and opioid addicts, while Pfizer Inc.'s Chantix pills block the brain's pleasure receptors activated when people smoke.

Small-molecule drugs like Chantix that function inside the brain can raise safety concerns. Chantix carries a federally mandated warning to users of possible depression and suicidal thoughts. A spokesman for Pfizer notes that no causal link between Chantix and such symptoms has been made.

By contrast, addiction-treatment vaccines work in the bloodstream, not the brain. Clinical trials have so far revealed no significant side effects, though the vaccines would do nothing to combat cravings. They work by tricking the body to reject drugs as if they are foreign pathogens. Normally, tiny drug molecules wend their way through the bloodstream to the brain, unleashing a flood of chemicals involved with pleasure and gratification. The drug molecules are too small to goad the immune system into generating antibodies to fight them off.

Scientists have figured out how to attach molecules similar to addictive drugs to much bigger antigens, such as deactivated versions of cholera or the common cold. When injected, these so-called conjugate vaccines spur the immune system to create antibodies to fight the

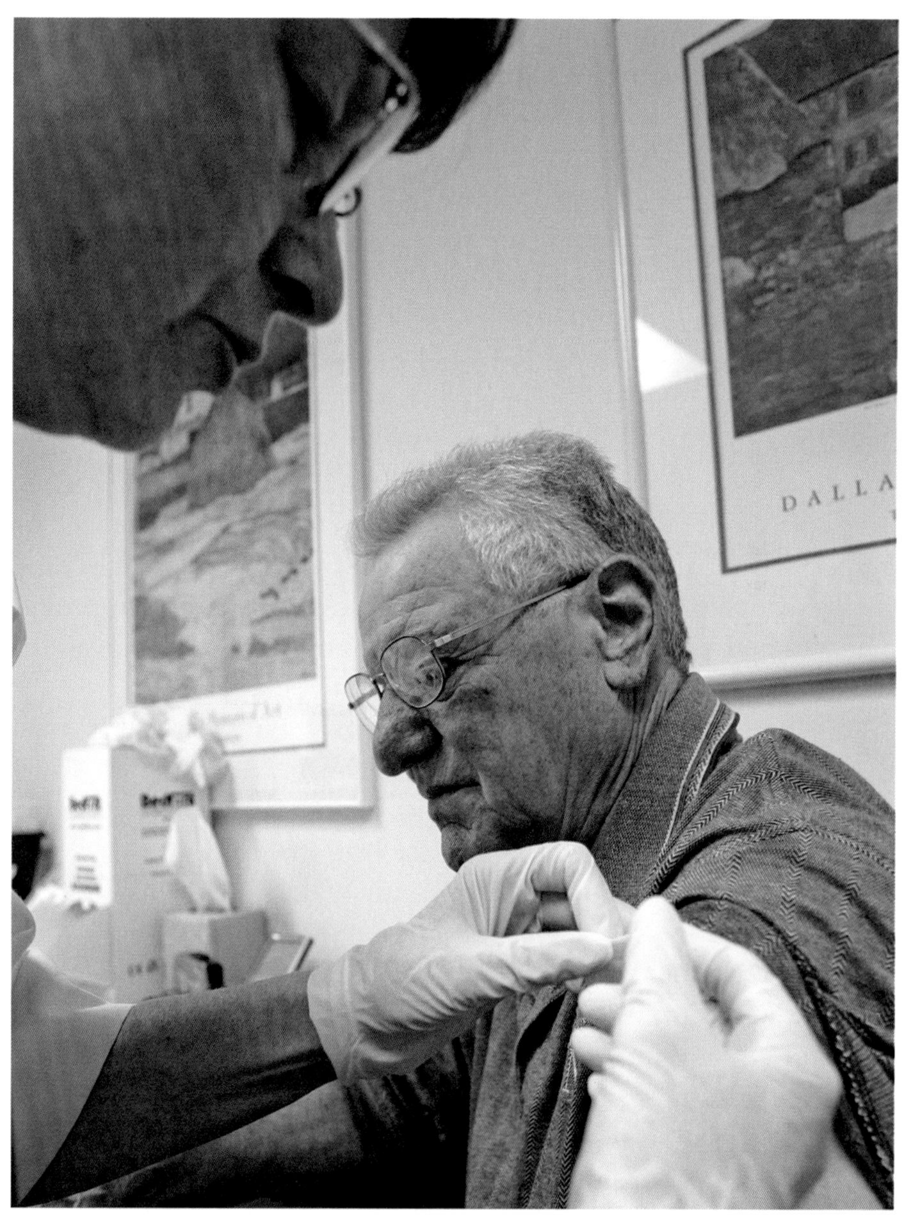

A man receives a nicotine vaccine. Most vaccines for addiction have targeted tobacco smoking, but vaccines for other abused substances are also being researched and developed.

tiny, addictive-drug molecules. These antibodies have in several studies glommed on to molecules of nicotine, cocaine and heroin ingested by lab animals and in some cases people, blocking them from triggering the pleasure centers in the brain.

"The antibody is like a sponge," says Kim Janda, a professor of chemistry and immunology at the Scripps Research Institute in La Jolla, Calif. "The drug comes in and it's soaked up, and you try to soak up as much as you can before it crosses the blood-brain barrier."

It could be years, if ever, before any vaccines to treat addiction reach the market. Failures have so far outnumbered successes, and big pharmaceutical companies haven't lent their research muscle to vaccines for illegal drugs.

"These vaccines have the potential to transform the way we treat drug addiction, but there are challenges," says Nora Volkow, the director of the National Institute on Drug Abuse.

A small Swedish firm, Independent Pharmaceutica AB, put its development of a nicotine vaccine on hold a year ago after it failed to outperform a placebo in trial. Convinced the concept of a nicotine vaccine remains sound, the company is now considering improvements to how the drug is delivered, says Lena Degling Wikingsson, a consultant and the company's former chief executive.

Another quit-smoking vaccine from Switzerland's Cytos Biotechnology—which has a licensing agreement with Novartis AG—failed to meet its endpoint in a 2009 trial. Work on that drug continues, however, with a new trial funded by the National Institutes of Health at Duke University in collaboration with Wake Forest University to test the vaccine in 65 smokers, Novartis says.

Stephen Evans-Freke, managing general partner of Bermuda-based private-equity firm Celtic Pharma Management, said a 2007 trial of a nicotine vaccine it owns "failed totally" because of a manufacturing error. He said the company could turn back to study the nicotine vaccine if a trial currently underway of the firm's TA-CD cocaine vaccine proves successful.

A vaccine isn't viable for treating alcoholism—among the costliest of addictions—because alcohol molecules are far too small to trigger the immune system, says Thomas Kosten, a pioneer of addiction-vaccine research at Baylor College of Medicine in Houston.

Most commercial vaccine-development efforts are focused on tobacco. Slightly more than a fifth of U.S. adults light up regularly.

Nearly half of U.S. smokers try to quit each year, but just 4% to 7% of quit attempts—most of them unaided—are successful long-term, according to American Lung Association estimates.

Just one out of three people trying to quit—at best—ends up kicking the habit for good, even with cessation aids, says Norman Edelman, the Association's chief medical officer and a professor of medicine at New York's Stony Brook University.

Nabi Biopharmaceuticals, a Rockville, Md., biotechnology company, is farthest down the path toward possible regulatory approval for an addiction vaccine, with two Phase III trials underway in several U.S. sites of its NicVAX product to help people quit smoking.

"The relapse is the biggest thing," says Raafat Fahim, the company's chief executive. "With antibodies staying a long period of time with you, it then protects you against the relapses."

Nabi in 2009 got a $10 million grant from NIDA, and sealed a licensing pact with the U.K.'s GlaxoSmithKline PLC that, including a $40 million up-front payment, could be worth up to $500 million, plus possible royalty payments.

Nabi's Phase II trial—the one Mr. Ballou participated in—found that smokers taking NicVAX were about three times as likely to be off cigarettes 44 weeks after vaccination than subjects given a placebo, Dr. Fahim says. That test was very small, and the results weren't as good as Pfizer got from a much larger Phase III trial of Chantix, he says. Subjects in Nabi's Phase III trial will get an extra dosage of NicVax compared to those in the Phase II trial.

One of the possible advantages of a vaccine, which would likely be used alongside psychological therapy and possibly other medications,

Fast Fact

A September 23, 2011, *Houston Chronicle* article reported that recent human trials of a cocaine vaccine found that the vaccine created high enough antibody levels in 70 percent of the vaccinated individuals to negate the effects of one to two doses of cocaine; 40 percent of the participants developed such heightened antibody levels that no amount of cocaine could produce a high for the user.

Anti-Addiction Vaccines in Development

Vaccine	Addiction Affected	Institution	Current Status
TA-CD	Cocaine	Celtic Pharma	Phase II clinical trials
TA-NIC	Nicotine	Celtic Pharma	Phase II clinical trials
NicVAX	Nicotine	Nabi Biopharmaceuticals/ GlaxoSmithKline	Phase III clinical trials
3 unnamed	Methamphetamine	Scripps Research	Laboratory research
Unnamed	Methamphetamine	InterveXion	Laboratory research

Taken from: Adapted from Xiaoyun Shen, Frank M. Orson, and Thomas R. Kosten. "Anit-Addiction Vaccines." *F1000 Medical Reports*, 2011.

is that it could require a once-a-month injection, as opposed to current anti-addiction medications that sometimes need to be taken several times a day.

"It's a lot easier to take a couple of vaccinations than to put on a patch every day, or keep chewing that nicotine gum, or doing whatever measures you're taking," says Phil Skolnick, director of the division of pharmacotherapies and medical consequences of drug abuse at NIDA.

Recent results from a test of an anticocaine vaccine in mice at Weill Cornell Medical College in New York were encouraging, researchers say.

"We give intravenous dosages of cocaine that's in excess of what humans take and it's like water to the mice" that have received the vaccine, says Ronald Crystal, the study's lead investigator and the chairman of genetic medicine at Weill Cornell. "They don't run around and get hyperactive." The researchers are now studying the vaccine in non-human primates.

Meanwhile, Dr. Kosten continues work on the TA-CD cocaine vaccine with a 300-subject, randomized, multi-site trial. Dr. Kosten says he hopes to report on the outcome of this trial sometime next year.

EVALUATING THE AUTHOR'S ARGUMENTS:

Mark Long reports on how anti-addiction vaccines may be helpful in weaning addicts off specific drugs. Given the failure rate so far, do you think this is a worthwhile pursuit in the overall fight against drug use and its consequences in America? Explain.

Vaccines Would Not Be an Effective Treatment for Drug Addiction

"Even the most effective anti-addiction vaccine can't cure the underlying factors that make people prone to using drugs."

Angela Garcia

Drug addiction is a mental and environmental problem as well as a biological craving, states Angela Garcia in the viewpoint that follows. Because of this, Garcia claims, efforts to produce vaccines to curb drug addiction can only address the physiological part of the condition and unfortunately ignore the personal and social factors that drive people to use drugs. Garcia insists that vaccines may help some people overcome specific addictions, but the root reasons for using drugs need to be addressed if the nation is going to successfully combat this cultural malady. Garcia is a professor of anthropology at Stanford University who has clinical experience in helping drug addicts.

Angela Garcia, "Heroin Vaccine Won't 'Cure' What Ails Addicts," *LA Times*, April 15, 2012.

AS YOU READ, CONSIDER THE FOLLOWING QUESTIONS:

1. As Garcia writes, approximately how long have researchers been working on vaccines to combat addictions?
2. Why did the employees at the clinic Garcia worked at scoff at the idea that they would one day acquire anti-addiction vaccines?
3. What are two of the ethical/legal issues that the author says will be raised by the potential implementation of anti-addiction vaccines?

My aunt Marion is in the hospital dying of liver and kidney failure, the result of her 20-year struggle with heroin use. I was told of her imminent death the same day news broke about a vaccine against the drug. "Breakthrough heroin vaccine could render drug 'useless' in addicts," one headline read. "Scientists create vaccine against heroin high," proclaimed another.

Meanwhile, my aunt finds temporary relief in the ever more frequent administration of opiate pain medication—the very kind of drugs she used illegally.

The idea of an anti-addiction vaccine is not new. For nearly 40 years scientists have been working on vaccines against all kinds of addictions, including nicotine, marijuana and alcohol. There are even trials of vaccines to prevent obesity. None of the anti-addiction vaccines has yet received Food and Drug Administration approval, however, and most of the studies are still in their early stages.

The headlines trumpeting a heroin vaccine were based on a finding that the drug had proved to be effective on mice during trials in Mexico (a nation that could use some good news related to drugs). Scientists now plan to test the patented vaccine in humans. If all goes well, the vaccine could be available in five years [by 2017]—too late for my aunt but providing a glimmer of hope for the estimated 1 million heroin addicts in the United States. Perhaps.

Vaccine Skepticism

Six years ago, when I was a doctoral student researching heroin addiction in northern New Mexico, I received an email from a scientist studying a possible vaccine against the drug's use. The study was in rat models, but early results were promising and suggested the likelihood of a therapeutic effect for humans. Aware of the devastating heroin epidemic in

New Mexico, which had the highest rate of heroin-related deaths in the United States, and of my work trying to understand it, the scientist wanted to offer some hope. He wrote that he could imagine a time when heroin addiction, in New Mexico and around the world, would be a thing of the past. I wanted to believe him, but I was less optimistic.

As an anthropologist with personal ties to the problem of addiction, I have studied the social and historical influences of drug use, and that has made me skeptical about the idea of a vaccine. Entrenched poverty, social inequality and personal despair all promote drug use, and these things profoundly shape the unequal outcomes of the addicted. Where I lived and worked, illicit drugs were more available than mental health services, and heroin was often used as a "medicine" to relieve the suffering of everyday life.

Fast Fact

In December 2007 the Robert Wood Johnson Foundation reported the findings of a study that found the root of addiction to be a physical, mental, and spiritual imbalance, and as a result, many current methods of treatment fail to help addicts recover because they do not employ holistic means that address an individual's multiple aspects.

On the afternoon of the scientist's email, I returned to the drug recovery clinic where I worked caring for patients undergoing heroin detox and described the idea of a vaccine against addiction to my colleagues. Jose, a drug counselor with a portrait of Jesus tattooed on his needle-scarred forearm, called it science fiction. Monica, the clinic's cook, doubted that such advances, if they actually materialized, would ever benefit the *tecatos* [Spanish slang for "drug user"] of northern New Mexico. She pointed out that the clinic could barely afford day-old tortillas, much less expensive new vaccines. We dismissed the idea and returned to addressing the day-to-day struggles of our heroin-addicted patients, many of them friends and family.

Vaccines Ignore the Reasons for Drug Use

The development of an anti-addiction vaccine still faces major challenges. In the past, vaccines that were effective in animal models have proved ineffective in humans. This is partly because the molecules introduced into the blood to generate antibodies against the effects of the drug on the brain are incredibly tiny. The human immune system is vastly more complex than that of the animals used for testing, and it tends to simply ignore the vaccine. Scientists are working their way around this problem by attaching proteins and chemicals to the molecules to induce antibody production. Such anti-addiction "vaccine cocktails," as they are ironically called, reflect the growing perception that addiction is a biologically based disease of the brain, making the very idea of a vaccine against addiction plausible.

One problem, though, is that even the most effective anti-addiction vaccine can't cure the underlying factors that make people prone to using drugs, including poverty, violence and lack of opportunity. Rather, the vaccines are aimed at preventing a drug user from experiencing the pleasure associated with a particular drug. When a mouse no longer feels pleasure from a drug because of a vaccine, it doesn't have the option of turning to another pleasure-producing substance. But humans do. A vaccine against pleasure derived from one kind of drug use might well spawn other forms of pleasure-seeking, especially when the drugs were being used in an attempt to relieve suffering.

The National Institute on Drug Abuse is pouring resources into the development of anti-addiction vaccines and their future use as medical

The author argues that vaccines that deflect pleasure derived from one kind of drug might well spawn other forms of addictive pleasure seeking.

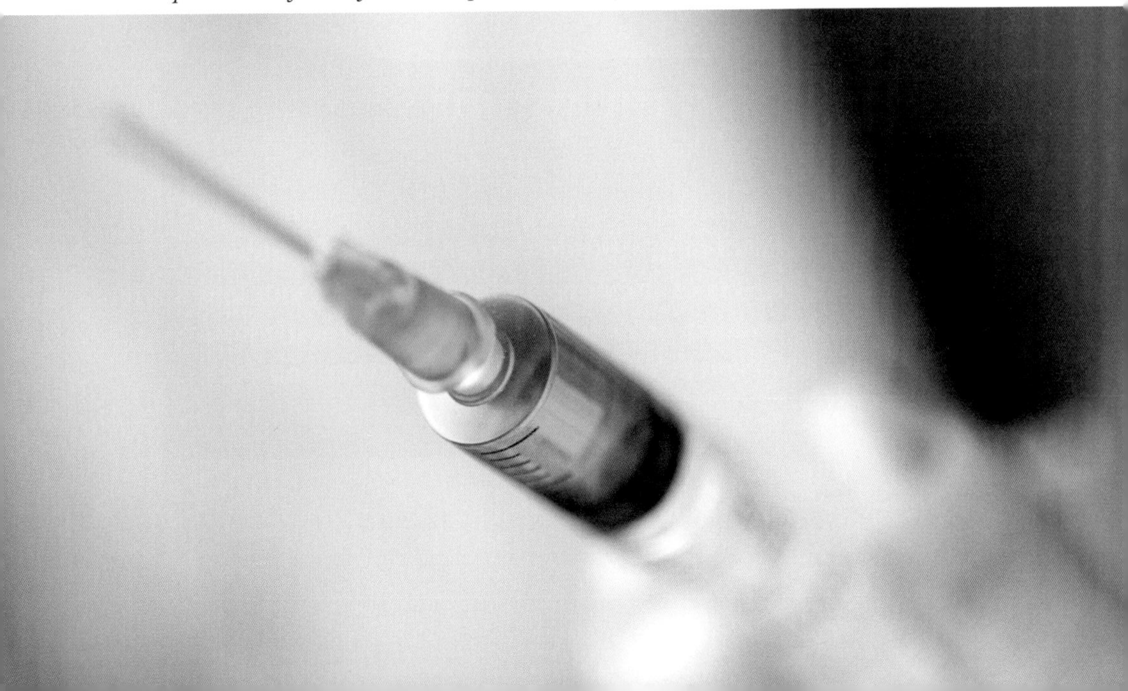

treatment. Should such vaccines one day become available, they may help some motivated individuals struggling to kick a particular substance, especially if coupled with other forms of treatment. But underlying issues of addiction causality, including inequality, hopelessness and the human desire for pleasure, cannot be addressed by a vaccine alone.

Unanswered Questions and Concerns

Moreover, a vaccine against pleasure and relief, however derived, raises worrying ethical and legal issues that deserve more scrutiny than is currently being given in media coverage on the anti-addiction vaccine "breakthrough." Will vaccine therapy be implemented through legal coercion, as much of rehab is today? Will addicts take dangerously high levels of drugs in an attempt to surpass the vaccine's effect and achieve a high? (This has been observed in anti-cocaine vaccine trials, in both mice and humans.) Will children of drug users be vaccinated?

In an Albuquerque hospital, my aunt is now receiving legally the opioids she so desperately sought on the streets. The family members that surround her hospital bed—the very ones that begged her to get clean—now ask her doctors to give her more drugs to ease her pain, and perhaps even offer her a hint of pleasure.

I am hopeful that we will one day have more effective therapies for the treatment of addiction. But in developing those treatments, we have to understand that for many addicts, the heroin or meth or cocaine or alcohol they abuse is more than an illicit drug. It is also medicine.

EVALUATING THE AUTHOR'S ARGUMENTS:

Compare Angela Garcia's viewpoint to the previous viewpoint by Mark Long. How do the two arguments address different aspects of the drug problem today? If you had to decide whether or not to fund drug vaccines, whose argument do you believe would more influence you decision? Why?

Chapter 2

What Types of Addiction Exist?

Addiction today seems to include more and more behaviors, including drugs, nicotine, alcohol, gambling, Internet and cell phone use, and overeating.

Teens Can Become Addicted to Nicotine More Quickly than Adults

"The design and contents of tobacco products make them extremely addictive."

Centers for Disease Control and Prevention

In the following viewpoint the Centers for Disease Control and Prevention (CDC) claims that parents need to prevent teens from using tobacco. The author claims that once teens start using tobacco, they can easily become addicted, which can lead to a lifetime of health issues. Tobacco products are designed for addiction and deliver nicotine faster and stronger than before. The CDC claims that youth are more sensitive to nicotine and can feel dependent on it faster than adults. The Centers for Disease Control and Prevention is a US government health agency.

AS YOU READ, CONSIDER THE FOLLOWING QUESTIONS:

1. What are some tobacco-related health problems?
2. What are some tobacco products currently on the market?
3. How many teen smokers end up smoking into adulthood, according to the article?

"Protecting Your Children from Tobacco Use," CDC.gov, August 6, 2012.

As the new school year approaches, parents and caregivers start thinking about preparing their children for the upcoming year. For parents of middle schoolers and teens, how to keep kids from using tobacco products might not seem as serious as other issues. In fact, some parents may feel that smoking is a "rite of passage" and that kids who start will outgrow the behavior as they get older. However, once teens start using tobacco, they can quickly become addicted, and that addiction can lead to a lifetime of serious health problems. The best way for parents to protect their children from tobacco-related health problems (including asthma, heart disease, cancer, and lung damage) is to prevent tobacco use altogether.

Tobacco Products Are Designed for Addiction

The design and contents of tobacco products make them extremely addictive. Products currently on the market include cigarettes, cigars, and smokeless tobacco (snuff, chewing tobacco, and dissolvable products). Today's tobacco products deliver more nicotine and deliver it quicker than ever before. Nicotine is the highly addictive drug in tobacco that keeps people using it, even when they want to quit. Like heroin and cocaine, nicotine changes the way the brain works—creating feelings of pleasure or satisfaction—and causing users to crave repeated doses of nicotine. Youth are especially sensitive to nicotine and can feel dependent earlier than adults. Because of their addiction, about three out of four teen smokers end up smoking into adulthood, even if they intend to quit after a few years.

Many tobacco products are flavored to make them more attractive to new users. While flavored cigarettes are now prohibited, tobacco companies still put fruit and candy flavors in many of their cigarette-sized cigars and in a variety of smokeless products. All of these products can cause serious health problems and lead to nicotine addiction and future smoking. And tobacco companies are still using techniques to make cigarettes taste less harsh—especially brands that most young people use when they start smoking.

The 2012 Surgeon General's report (Preventing Tobacco Use Among Youth and Young Adults—A Report of the Surgeon General) says that young people sometimes use smokeless tobacco products in places where cigarettes are banned, such as schools. Snus (dry snuff in a pouch) and dissolvable smokeless products in particular provide a way for smokers to maintain their addiction to nicotine, even when they can't smoke. In fact, most young people who use these smokeless products also smoke cigarettes. These products are dangerous because they can introduce kids to nicotine, putting them at risk for nicotine addiction.

The following sections summarize other key messages from the 2012 Surgeon General's report. Also provided are resources to help prevent youth from using tobacco or being exposed to secondhand smoke as well as helpful quit resources.

Tobacco Products Cause Serious Harm, Even to Young People

Most people know that tobacco use can lead to disease and death in long-term, older smokers, but many are surprised to learn how early the negative impacts of tobacco use can occur. It's important that parents know how early smoking can lead to nicotine addiction, early heart disease, and lung damage.

> **FAST FACT**
>
> **Although one cigarette contains just ten milligrams of nicotine, and a smoker will ingest only one to two milligrams per cigarette, these small amounts have been shown to be enough to cause someone to become addicted to the drug, according to the National Institute on Drug Abuse.**

Addiction to tobacco can happen at any age, but the younger they start using tobacco, the more likely youth will become addicted and the stronger their addiction will be.

Most young smokers already show signs of cardiovascular damage. For example, the large blood vessel that feeds oxygen to the body's major organs—the abdominal aorta—shows thickening of the walls through which blood passes to the rest of the body and already can contain fatty streaks in smokers as young as 15 or 16 years of age.

Early smoking can lead to permanent lung damage. In addition to reducing lung function, smoking slows down lung growth.

Studies have shown that teens become addicted to nicotine faster than adults do.

Because lungs continue growing and developing until young men and women reach their early 20s, youth who smoke may never develop full lung size or capacity. Such damage is permanent and increases the risk for chronic obstructive pulmonary disease (COPD) later in life.

What Is in a Cigarette?

Substance	Normal Use of Substance
Acetone	Solvent
Ammoniac	Detergent
Arsenic	Lethal poison
Cadmium*	Used in batteries
Carbon monoxide	Found in exhaust fumes
Cyanhydric acid	Was used in Holocaust gas chambers
DDT	Insecticide
Dibenzacridine*	
Methanol	Used as rocket fuel
Naphtalene	Moth repellent
Naphtylamine*	
Nicotine	Used as an herbicide and insecticide
Polonium 210*	A radioactive element
Pyrene*	
Toluene	Industrial solvent
Urethane*	
Vinyl chloride	Used in plastic materials

*Known carcinogenic substances

Taken from: *State of the Environment.* Tasmanian Planning Commission, Government of Australia.

Why Do Youth Use Tobacco?

The reasons young people begin to use tobacco include:

- Tobacco industry marketing. Tobacco companies spend more than a million dollars an hour, 24 hours a day, 7 days a week, to market their deadly products. Even though the tobacco industry is no longer allowed to target children with advertising and promotions, youth are regularly exposed to images suggesting that tobacco use is cool, adult, and appealing. This marketing, including coupons and other

promotions that make cigarettes more affordable, directly contributes to the number of young people who smoke.
- Social influences. Adolescents are more likely to try tobacco if they see tobacco use as a normal behavior because their friends or family members use tobacco.
- Physical influences. Nicotine is just as addictive as heroin and cocaine. Because teens are sensitive to nicotine, they can feel dependent on tobacco sooner than adults.
- Environmental influences. If teens and young adults are exposed to images that portray smokers as cool, attractive, rebellious, fun loving, risk taking, or other characteristics they admire, they may want to smoke, too. Such images are often found in advertising displays at convenience stores and other outlets that sell tobacco, as well as in movies and on TV.

Who Is at Greatest Risk?

Young people are more likely to use tobacco if they:

- Have access to smoking areas and tobacco products—especially low-cost or free tobacco
- Have friends or siblings who use tobacco
- Watch movies that have smoking in them
- Are not doing well in school or have friends who are not doing well in school
- Are not engaged in school or religious activities
- Use other substances, such as alcohol or marijuana

What Your Community Can Do to Help Prevent Youth Tobacco Use

Following are some state and national policies proven to work best:

- Make tobacco products less affordable
- Restrict tobacco marketing
- Ban smoking in public places—such as workplaces, schools, day care centers, hospitals, restaurants, hotels, and parks

How You Can Help Your Children Stay Tobacco-Free

With so many high-risk activities available in today's culture, parenting adolescents can sometimes feel overwhelming. However, the risks associated with smoking—and with other tobacco use that often leads to smoking—are just as overwhelming. Despite decades of health warnings, 46 million Americans still smoke cigarettes today. More than 70% of them want to quit, but nicotine addiction is so powerful, quitting is very difficult and many smokers just give up trying. Nearly half a million die from smoking every year—an average of 13 years earlier than their peers who don't smoke—and for every smoker who dies, 20 more live with at least one serious chronic disease caused by smoking. More than 3.6 million middle school and high school students smoke cigarettes; one out of three teen smokers will ultimately die from a tobacco-related disease. That is not a future parents want for their children. The key is prevention, because nearly 90% of smokers start smoking before they're 18 and almost no one starts after age 25. To help keep your children from starting to use tobacco, take these important steps:

- Tell your children emphatically and often how dangerous smoking is—and how addictive all tobacco products are.
- Make your home and your car tobacco-free for everyone—friends and guests as well as family members.
- Tell your children you expect them to be tobacco-free.
- Ask your child's doctor to discuss health issues caused by tobacco use—including nicotine addiction.
- Encourage your children to be involved in activities at school, church, or in the community.
- Don't let your children see movies, TV programming, or video games that show tobacco use.
- Find out where your community stands on policies known to reduce tobacco use by youth, such as school-based tobacco bans, smoke-free policies, and higher prices on tobacco products.
- Set a good example by not using tobacco yourself.

EVALUATING THE AUTHOR'S ARGUMENTS:

The Centers for Disease Control and Prevention (CDC) is a US government health agency. Do you think this credential helps make the CDC's argument that teens are more susceptible to tobacco valid? Why or why not?

Nicotine Is Not Instantly Addictive

"How plausible is it that someone who has smoked exactly one cigarette in his life has tried to quit smoking but couldn't?"

Jacob Sullum

Researchers who claim that nicotine is instantly addictive to teens are surely misguided, claims Jacob Sullum in the following viewpoint. Sullum, a senior editor at *Reason* magazine, argues that common sense certainly shows that smoking one cigarette is not likely to turn teens into nicotine addicts, and he cites other researchers who insist that most teens who experiment with smoking will not become smokers. What worries Sullum, though, is that the message touting instant addiction may overshadow other supportable concerns such as the health risks associated with smoking.

AS YOU READ, CONSIDER THE FOLLOWING QUESTIONS:

1. Why is Sullum suspicious of the phrase "very soon after the first cigarette" in the statement by DiFranza?
2. According to the studies done in New Zealand, as cited by the author, how many adolescent smokers revealed that they experienced a "loss of autonomy" after completing DiFranza's checklist?
3. In Sullum's opinion, how does Jane Brody contradict herself in her *New York Times* article on nicotine addiction?

Jacob Sullum, " Hooked on the Myth of Instantly Addictive Cigarettes," Reason.com, February 13, 2008.

Digging through a pile of medical journals, *New York Times* health reporter Jane Brody discovers that cigarettes are instantly addictive:

Dire warning to all adolescents: You can get "hooked from the first cigarette."

Brody is quoting an article from the December [2007] *Journal of Family Practice* in which tobacco researcher Joseph R. DiFranza warns that "one cigarette may be all it takes to get hooked." But DiFranza immediately back-pedals:

Hooked from the first cigarette?

You bet.

Very soon after that first cigarette, adolescents can experience a loss of autonomy over tobacco, and recent research indicates that this loss of autonomy may play a key role in nicotine addiction.

Notice how the claim of instant addiction quickly becomes a claim that some time after the first cigarette (possibly after the 10th or 100th?) smokers may begin to experience "loss of autonomy," which ultimately could play a role in addiction.

The "Loss of Autonomy" Checklist

And how is this "loss of autonomy" measured? With a 10-point checklist:

1. Have you ever tried to quit smoking, but couldn't?
2. Do you smoke *now* because it is really hard to quit?
3. Have you ever felt like you were addicted to tobacco?
4. Do you ever have strong cravings to smoke?
5. Have you ever felt like you really needed a cigarette?
6. Is it hard to keep from smoking in places where you are not supposed to, like school?

When you tried to stop smoking (or, when you haven't used tobacco for a while):

7. Did you find it hard to concentrate because you couldn't smoke?
8. Did you feel more irritable because you couldn't smoke?
9. Did you feel a strong need or urge to smoke?
10. Did you feel nervous, restless, or anxious because you couldn't smoke?

If you answer yes to one or more of these questions, according to DiFranza, you have experienced "loss of autonomy" and are well on your way to a cigarette habit that will give you lung cancer when you're 65. In a sentence that Brody quotes, DiFranza says "three New Zealand national surveys involving 25,722 adolescent smokers who used this checklist revealed a loss of autonomy in 25% to 30% of young people who had smoked their one and only cigarette during the

A smoker reviews a "loss of autonomy" list as part of a smoking cessation program. The author says such lists are misleading.

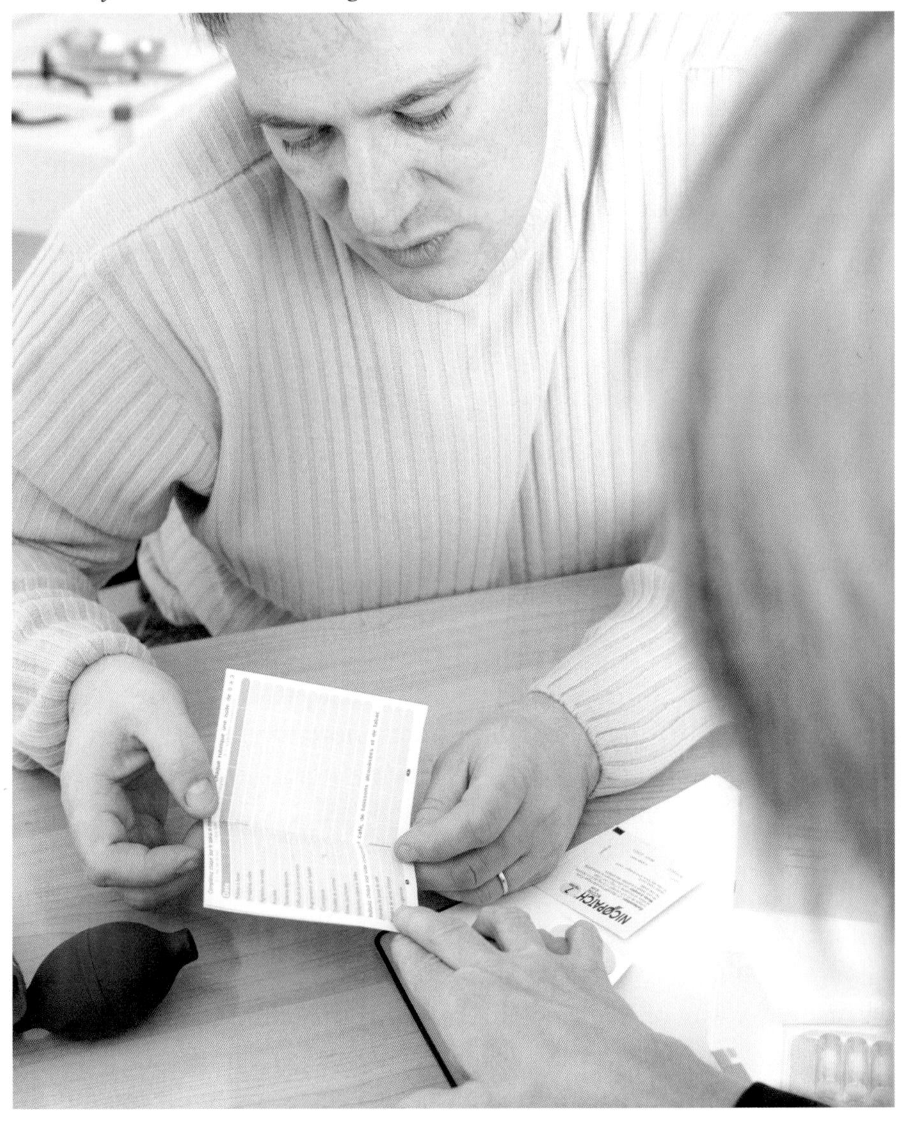

preceding month." How plausible is it that someone who has smoked exactly one cigarette in his life has tried to quit smoking but couldn't, or feels strong cravings for a cigarette, or gets irritable and has trouble concentrating when he can't smoke? Maybe teenagers who have tried cigarettes sometimes say such things because they believe that's what a smoker would say, and they are experimenting with that identity. Or maybe they are just screwing with the people conducting the survey.

Overeager Endorsements

Neither DiFranza nor Brody considers these possibilities. Brody is so eager to believe in the overwhelming power of nicotine that she does not even notice how she contradicts herself. After quoting a tobacco researcher who notes that "the vast majority of teenagers who try one or two cigarettes don't go on to become smokers," Brody blithely asserts that "smoking by youngsters . . . typically leads to a lifetime of smoking."

> **FAST FACT**
>
> **According to the National Institute on Drug Abuse's 2011 Monitoring the Future survey, which measures the drug use of 8th, 10th, and 12th graders, cigarette smoking among these groups has dropped to historically low levels. Smoking rates were reported at 18.7 percent of 12th graders, 11.8 percent of 10th graders, and 6.1 percent of 8th graders.**

This sort of misrepresentation reinforces the myth that nicotine is irresistible and inescapable, which is counterproductive for at least two reasons that DiFranza and Brody should be able to appreciate. Teenagers who experiment with tobacco or observe peers who do so will quickly discover that addiction takes more than a single cigarette. Having seen through the scare tactics aimed at stopping them from taking that first puff, they may be inclined to dismiss better-grounded concerns about, say, the long-term health consequences of a pack-a-day habit or the difficulty of giving up cigarettes once you've come to depend on them as a way of relieving stress. And if they do eventually become regular smokers, exaggerating the enslaving power of nicotine will discourage them from trying to quit and from persisting in the attempt.

EVALUATING THE AUTHOR'S ARGUMENTS:

How does Jacob Sullum's argument differ from that of the Centers for Disease Control and Prevention, author of the preceding viewpoint? Whose viewpoint do you think is the more persuasive? Explain why.

Food Addiction Is a Real Addiction

Michael Prager

"'There are important similarities between overeating . . . and the classic addictions.'"

For much of his life, Michael Prager was obese because, as he claims, he was addicted to food. Prager writes in the following viewpoint about his addiction and the millions of Americans who are compulsive eaters. Drawing support from research studies that suggest food consumption stimulates pleasure centers in the brain, he insists that the addiction is real if, sadly, overlooked. Prager, a writer living in Virginia, asserts that many obese people would not choose to be so heavy nor bear the public ridicule; therefore he hopes that science, the medical profession, and society at large will focus more attention on getting food addicts the help they need.

AS YOU READ, CONSIDER THE FOLLOWING QUESTIONS:

1. How does Prager draw a link between the reception of alcoholism in the 1930s and food addiction today?
2. What brain chemical receptor is likely involved in overeating and obesity, according to the author?
3. What does Prager think should be a priority of lawmakers if they hope to address the nation's obesity epidemic?

Michael Prager, "Obesity and the Addiction to Food," *Boston Globe*, January 20, 2009.

No one needs another government study to know that America is drowning in an ocean of adipose [fat], so the state's anti-obesity initiative announced Jan. 8 [2009] is a welcome step. But it ignores the most basic fact about why so many Americans are fat and getting fatter.

That fact is food addiction.

An Often-Ignored Addiction

To many, this omission won't seem odd, for it is true that the medical establishment has not yet officially acknowledged the links between foods and addiction, and popular culture still thinks fat people are just weak and lazy and ought to just straighten themselves out.

The author contends that people can become addicted to food.

Until the mid-'30s, folks said the same thing about drunks, but then, as now, it was just ignorance talking. It is well accepted today that alcohol, drugs, and many other substances affect some people far more severely than others, and that sufferers are sick, not bad.

That change in attitude did not originate in science, but has come to be proven by research, and it will undoubtedly surprise many that science has already begun to catch up on the matter of food addiction, in the form of hundreds of peer-reviewed studies.

Among the most impressive studies is the brain-imaging work conducted in 2004 at the McKnight Brain Center at University of Florida, which suggests "there are important similarities between overeating highly palatable and hedonic foods and the classic addictions."

A study published in 1994 found that the brain's D2 dopamine receptor, already implicated in alcoholism, is also involved with obesity and with cocaine and tobacco dependence. And just last month [in December 2008], Princeton psychology professor Bart Hoebel presented research to the American College of Neuropsychopharmacology that suggests sugar is an addictive substance.

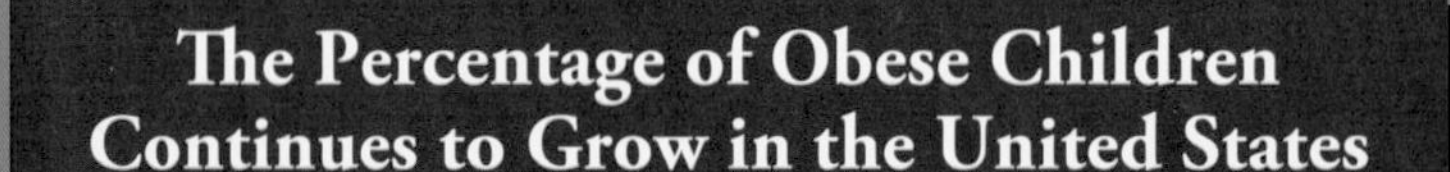

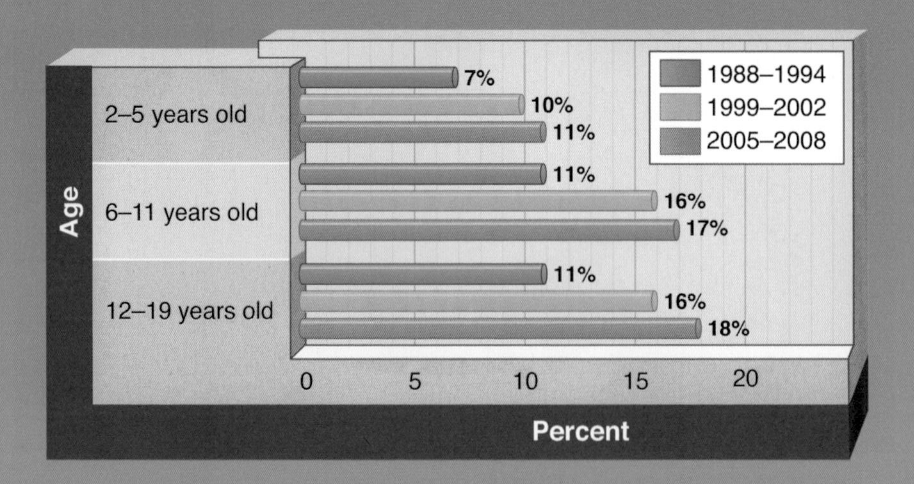

Taken from: *U.S. News & World Report.* "Childhood Obesity: Nation's Children Growing in the Wrong Direction," March 23, 2011. www.usnews.com.

Beyond pure research, a growing cadre of nutritionists, counselors, and clinicians are facilitating and witnessing patients' long-term success by applying the methods that have helped other addicts. Some of their leaders will gather this week [late January 2009] in Houston for the first International Conference of Food Addiction Professionals.

Personal Experience with Food Addiction

Though I believe in science, I became convinced about food addiction in the most personal way possible: I was severely obese for most of my first 33 years, and weighed 365 pounds on Oct. 21, 1991, the day I was admitted to the eating disorders unit of South Oaks Hospital, an accredited psychiatric hospital on Long Island [New York].

During a nine-week stay, my counselors deployed the same methods their counterparts were using in the alcohol wards across the green, at the gambling ward around the corner, and elsewhere in the hospital. The treatment cost $54,000, but what insurance didn't cover, the hospital waived, and my life was saved: I've been living in sanity, serenity, and a normal-sized body for better than 15 years.

The insurance angle is a key part of the story. For several reasons, including the advent of managed care, coverage essentially is no longer available, even while insurers helped pay the estimated $4.4 billion in bariatric-surgery costs last year. Changing that inequity should be a priority of lawmakers if they want to make a dent in the obesity epidemic. Certainly, not everyone who is overweight is an addict, but the more overweight people are, the more likely that they have crossed the line from big eater to habitual user. And it is the most obese people who need the most disproportionate share of medical resources.

Fast Fact

In an August 2011 *Archives of General Psychiatry* article, the authors cite research that functional magnetic resonance imaging has shown that the consumption of food and drugs initiates reward responses in the same regions of the brain; additional research cited found that food and drug cravings also occur in the same regions of the brain.

Not Acting in Their Right Minds

If there isn't enough money to support both treatments, obviously the surgical option should go. Most people didn't get fat because their stomachs could hold too much food, and surgically shrinking stomachs isn't going to address the emotional and spiritual deficits that drive most overeaters.

Instead of seeing a fat person and thinking, "How could he let himself go like that?" it might be better to ask, "Did he have any choice?" Would anyone in his right mind endure so much discomfort, not to mention public shame?

That's what addicts do, engage in activities they know are killing them. In short, not acting in their right minds. There's help for that.

EVALUATING THE AUTHOR'S ARGUMENTS:

Michael Prager insists that insurance coverage for food addiction is essential if obese people are to get help. After reading this viewpoint, do you agree that medical insurance should cover food addiction? Why or why not?

Food Addiction Is Not a Real Addiction

Richard Berman

"We are no more addicted to food than we are addicted to air or to water."

In the following viewpoint Richard Berman, the president of a public relations and lobbying firm in Washington, D.C., contends that craving food is not an addiction. He maintains that science does not support the notion of food addiction nor does the commonsense observation that people cannot be addicted to something they need for survival. Berman states that the desire to tout food as an addictive temptation stems from society's willingness to overlook the role of personal responsibility as a remedy to any kind of overindulgence.

AS YOU READ, CONSIDER THE FOLLOWING QUESTIONS:

1. What is the twofold argument that activists use to attack food as addictive, according to Berman?
2. As Berman explains, what "amplification"—originally asserted by the Centers for Disease Control and Prevention—has helped support erroneous claims that food is addictive?
3. What is the Yale "food addiction scale," as the author describes it?

Richard Berman, "Industry Must Stop Activists' Food-as-Addiction Attacks," *Nation's Restaurant News,* vol. 46, no. 12, June 11, 2012.

If anti-food-industry activists have their way, "chili cheeseburger" eventually will be synonymous with "crack cocaine."

The new theory suggests that a restaurant is little better than a meth dealer, hooking customers on addictive foods—"bet you can't eat just one"—cooked up by an evil genius in a laboratory. Is your company adding sugar to cereals? You might as well be peddling heroin on the playground.

Hyping Temptation as Addiction

For the last decade these activists have laid the groundwork needed to convince consumers and legislators that food processors are driving a nationwide "addiction" to food.

Their attack is twofold.

The first step is to convince the public that personal responsibility is an impossibility in the face of the temptation created by "hyper-palatable" choices on store shelves and restaurant menus. The second step is to convince people this temptation is clinical, thus necessitating government interference to curb it.

Margo Wootan of the Center for Science in the Public Interest laid out the case back in 2004 when she observed that "we've got to move beyond personal responsibility." Kelly Brownell of Yale University's Rudd Center for Food Policy & Obesity once described personal responsibility as "an experiment that has failed," adding, "We believe that there is sufficient science to suggest there is something to this [food addiction]."

News reports breathlessly ask, "Are cupcakes as addictive as cocaine?"

Fast Fact

In reviewing the literature on functional magnetic resonance imaging relating to the consumption of food and brain reaction, authors of an April 2012 *Nature Reviews Neuroscience* article found a lack of consistency in the brain's response to food cues, suggesting that while there may be a neurological basis for food disorders such as binge eating or obesity, it has not been shown thus far to be as consistent as that of drug abuse.

"Self-help book cartoon. How to Stop Over-Consuming," cartoon by Chris Madden. Copyright © 2005 by Chris Madden. Reproduced by permission.

Of course, we laugh at the trial lawyers who sue fast-food outlets for making their clients fat, and respond with outrage when nanny-staters [those believed to support a government that overprotects its citizens] try to take toys out of kids' meals. But these reactions will become far rarer if we allow activists to create the impression that food addiction is real.

Unsupported Assertions Persist

Historically, ideas—even ridiculous or false ones—repeated often enough tend to take on a life of their own. For example, the U.S.

Centers for Disease Control and Prevention produced a study a few years back that claimed 400,000 people died each year from obesity—a number you still sometimes see cited. The only problem with that study? It's bunk. A follow-up published in the *Journal of the American Medical Association* found the number was only about one-quarter of the original estimate.

But the larger number got repeated over and over again, thanks to the amplification power of a small niche of public health groups. And most in the food industry were slow to rebut the claims. Before you knew it, obesity took the place of tobacco as the current public health crisis.

On the issue of food as addiction, similarly unsound "facts" are being pushed. For example, Yale academics have created a "food addiction scale" that mimics the criteria needed to meet the American Psychiatric Association Manual of Mental Disorders. If a subject meets three of the seven listed criteria, he or she is considered "dependent" on food. One Yale researcher found 11.4 percent of those she interviewed met the "food dependence" standard, writing that "even if food isn't addictive, we can all agree that certain foods have more abuse potential; they're more likely to be used in a problematic way than others."

The fact that we're even discussing the consumption of food—something we all do every day to keep from starving to death—as "abuse" signals where this debate is headed. And this is not a path we should allow the discussion to travel on any further. It ends with trial lawyers and warnings.

Personal Responsibility Must Prevail

On the one hand, there's the rhetorical response: We are no more addicted to food than we are addicted to air or to water. We need these things to survive. It's time to remind America of its love affair with personal responsibility.

We also must attack the "science" of food addiction. A researcher from Swansea University in Wales found "no evidence from the human literature for the hypothesis that sucrose may be physically addictive." As one psychiatrist noted in *USA Today* a few years back, "If lawyers can turn fast food into an addiction and pin liability on restaurants, it won't be long before adulterers sue *Sports Illustrated*, claiming its swimsuit issue led them astray."

EVALUATING THE AUTHOR'S ARGUMENTS:

In the previous viewpoint Michael Prager argues that some people are "habitual users" of food and deserve medical help. Richard Berman, however, asserts in this viewpoint that to label food as an addictive substance is to ignore the role of personal responsibility in making commonsense choices. Do you believe that individuals can become addicted to food or that they simply have chosen to forsake moderation? Explain your answer by citing from the articles.

Viewpoint 5

Cell Phone Addiction Threatens People's Work and Personal Lives

"The faster smartphones become and the more alluring the apps that are devised for them, the stronger the addiction will grow."

The Economist

Smartphones and other instant communication devices are now commonplace in society. So too is a growing dependence on these technologies, argues the *Economist*, a British news publication that avoids author bylines to promote a unified voice. The publication claims that people have become slaves to their smartphones, living and working in a state of "hyperconnectivity" that leaves less time for other pursuits or even quiet reflection. The *Economist* contends that the lure of hyperconnectivity is an addiction that unfortunately compels people to live spur-of-the-moment, ever at the whim of the next important text message or email. The publication believes as smart devices evolve, the addiction will be harder to fight, and therefore users and creators must respond to the problem by encouraging "digital dieting."

"Slaves to the Smartphone," *The Economist*, vol. 402, no. 8775, March 10, 2012, p. 80.

AS YOU READ, CONSIDER THE FOLLOWING QUESTIONS:

1. According to Martin Lindstrom, quoted by the *Economist*, where did the sound of a vibrating smartphone rank on the list of the most powerfully affecting sounds that people recognize?
2. Why is hyperconnectivity destabilizing to the workplace, in the *Economist*'s view?
3. As the author explains, how did the Boston Consulting Group try to manage its employees' hyperconnectivity problem?

"The Servant" (1963) is one of those films that it is impossible to forget—a merciless dissection of the relationship between a scheming valet (played by Dirk Bogarde) and his dissolute master (James Fox). The valet exploits his master's weaknesses until he turns the tables: the story ends with a cringing Fox ministering to a lordly Bogarde. The film was an indictment of the class structure of [then prime minister] Harold Macmillan's Britain. But it is hard to watch it today without thinking of another fraught relationship—the one between businessfolk and their smartphones.

The Servant Has Become the Master

Smart devices are sometimes empowering. They put a world of information at our fingertips. They free people to work from home instead of squeezing onto a train with malodorous strangers. That is a huge boon for parents seeking flexible work hours. Smartphones and tablets can also promote efficiency by allowing people to get things done in spare moments that would otherwise be wasted, such as while queuing [waiting in line] for coffee. They can even help slackers create the illusion that they are working around the clock, by programming their e-mail to be sent at 1 A.M.

But for most people the servant has become the master. Not long ago only doctors were on call all the time. Now everybody is. Bosses think nothing of invading their employees' free time. Work invades the home far more than domestic chores invade the office. Otherwise-sane people check their smartphones obsessively, even during pre-dinner drinks, and send e-mails first thing in the morning and last thing at night.

This is partly because smartphones are addictive: when Martin Lindstrom, a branding guru, tried to identify the ten sounds that affect people most powerfully, he found that a vibrating phone came [in] third, after the Intel chime and a giggling baby. BlackBerrys and iPhones provide relentless stimuli interspersed with rewards. Whenever you check the glowing rectangle, there is a fair chance you will see a message from a client, a herogram [message of appreciation] from your boss or at least an e-mail from a Nigerian gentleman offering you $1m[illion] if you share your bank details with him. Smartphones are the best excuse yet devised

The Economist *claims that smartphones are addictive and their users have come to live in a state of hyper connectivity that precludes other pursuits.*

for procrastination. How many people can honestly say that they have never pruned their e-mails to put off tackling more demanding tasks?

Disappearing Downtime

Hyperconnectivity exaggerates some of the most destabilising trends in the modern workplace: the decline of certainty (as organisations abandon bureaucracy in favour of adhocracy [responding to problems as they arise, rather than planning for them]), the rise of global supply chains and the general cult of flexibility. Smartphones make it easier for managers to change their minds at the last moment: for example, to e-mail a minion at 11 P.M. to tell him he must fly to Pittsburgh tomorrow. The dratted devices also make it easier for managers in one time zone to spoil the evenings of managers in another.

Fast Fact

The June 2012 Mobile Mindset Study released by the company that created the Lookout Mobile Security app to help smartphone users protect their phones, found that 58 percent of individuals with smartphones check their devices a minimum of once every hour, and when asked about how they felt when they lost their phones, smartphone users reported feeling panicked (73 percent), desperate (14 percent), and sick (7 percent), with only 6 percent reporting feelings of relief.

Employees find it ever harder to distinguish between "on-time" and "off-time"—and indeed between real work and make-work. Executives are lumbered with two overlapping workdays: a formal one full of meetings and an informal one spent trying to keep up with the torrent of e-mails and messages.

None of this is good for businesspeople's marriages or mental health. It may be bad for business, too. When bosses change their minds at the last minute, it is hard to plan for the future. And several studies have shown what ought to be common sense: that people think more deeply if they are not constantly distracted.

Digital Dieting

What can be done to keep smartphones in their place? How can we reap the benefits of connectivity without becoming its slaves? One solution is digital dieting. Just as the abundance of junk food means

Daily Communication Methods of American Teens

The percentage of teens who contact their friends daily by different methods, by type

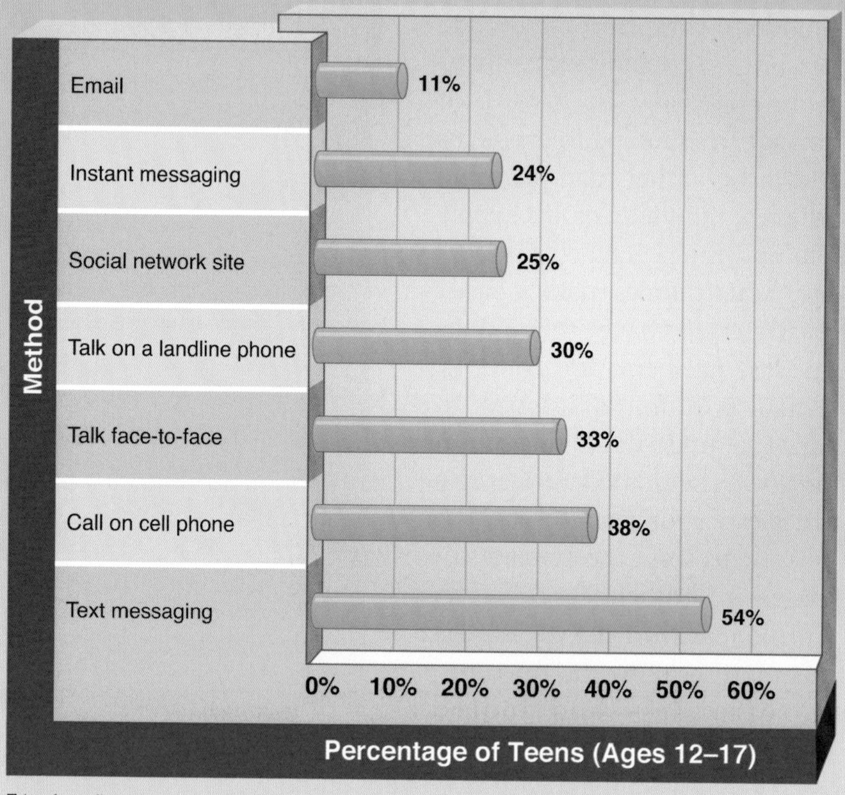

Taken from: Amanda Lenhart. "Teens, Cell Phones and Texting." Pew Research Center, April 20, 2012. http://pewresearch.org.

that people have to be more disciplined about their eating habits, so the abundance of junk information means they have to be more disciplined about their browsing habits. Banning browsing before breakfast can reintroduce a modicum of civilisation. Banning texting at weekends or, say, on Thursdays, can really show the iPhone who is boss.

The problem with this approach is that it works only if you live on a desert island or at the bottom of a lake. In "Sleeping with Your Smartphone", a forthcoming book, Leslie Perlow of Harvard Business School argues that for most people the only way to break the 24/7 habit is to act collectively rather than individually. She tells the story of how one of the world's most hard-working organisations, the Boston Consulting Group, learned to manage hyperconnectivity better. The firm introduced rules about when people were expected to be offline, and encouraged them to work together to make this possible. Many macho consultants mocked the exercise at first—surely only wimps switch off their smartphones? But eventually it forced people to work more productively while reducing burnout.

The Addiction Will Only Get Worse

Ms Perlow's advice should be taken seriously. The problem of hyperconnectivity will only get worse, as smartphones become smarter and young digital natives take over the workforce. People are handing ever more of their lives over to their phones, just as James Fox handed ever more of his life over to Dirk Bogarde. You can now download personal assistants (such as Apple's Siri) that tell you what is on your schedule, and virtual personal trainers that urge you [to] take more exercise. Ofcom, Britain's telecommunications regulator, says that a startling 60% of teenagers who use smartphones describe themselves as "highly addicted" to their devices. So do 37% of adults.

The faster smartphones become and the more alluring the apps that are devised for them, the stronger the addiction will grow. Spouses can help by tossing the darned devices out of a window or into a bucket of water. But ultimately it is up to companies to outsmart the smartphones by insisting that everyone turn them off from time to time.

EVALUATING THE AUTHOR'S ARGUMENTS:

The *Economist* suggests that one way to fight against cell phone addiction is to go on a "digital diet" and restrict use. Do you believe such "dieting"—whether collectively or individually motivated—is feasible in today's hyperconnected world? Explain why or why not.

Viewpoint 6

The Myth of Cell-Phone Addiction

"Instead of seeking to understand [the cultural change brought on by cell phone use], the temptation is to reach into pop culture's bag of ideological bromides and decry it as some sort of pathology."

Jeffrey A. Tucker

Jeffrey A. Tucker is the head of Laissez-Faire Books, a publisher of works on economic and social liberty. He is also an editorial consultant to the Ludwig von Mises Institute, an organization that supports a free marketplace. In the following viewpoint Tucker disputes the notion that people have become addicted to cell phone technology. On the contrary, Tucker insists that these modern wonders are allowing people the freedom to connect with others whenever and wherever they please. He believes naysayers commonly criticize anything that promotes personal freedom, and he notes that the government also tends to fear such unregulated freedoms. Tucker concludes that critics should mind their own business when it comes to the personal use of marketplace technologies.

Jeffrey A. Tucker, "The Myth of Cell-Phone Addiction," Ludwig Von Mises Institute, June 17, 2005.

AS YOU READ, CONSIDER THE FOLLOWING QUESTIONS:

1. Who, according to Tucker, has the right to ban cell phone use?
2. What was phone behavior like before the arrival of cell phone technology, as Tucker describes it?
3. To what other "freedom technology" does Tucker compare cell phones?

Pundits and bloggers are addicted to decrying the supposed cell-phone addiction of Americans. (1, 2, 3, 4, 5, 6, 7, 8, 9, 10, and 11). Calls for government to do something about it can't be far behind, especially considering the other claims that cell phones give us tumors, gut our memories, and jackhammer our brains. There are even reports of second-hand damage from others' cell phone use.

These articles go beyond merely claiming that cell phones are annoying—and truly people could learn some manners here, as in many other aspects of life. As regards this supposed "addiction"—this is a word attached to any habitual behaviors of others we do not like.

What's interesting here are those who offer something like a Marxian-style critique of cell-phone use. We are alienated from society, we are told, and obviously tormented by loneliness, and thereby seek solidarity and community. But rather than seek out genuine connection to others, we reach for technology, the very thing that alienated us to begin with. We grow ever more dependent on our gizmos but they ultimately disappoint because they only cause addiction to machines and thereby increase alienation.

Also, we the oppressed long for empowerment and the ego-boost generated by the sense of importance granted by the idea of receiving and sending cell-phone calls. We can't stop using our cell-phones and yet they only further entangle us in an artificial world of machines created via the money matrix.

Oh just look at the cell-phone people everywhere! Surely this is the final stage of capitalism in which we ignore our brothers and sisters walking next to us but instead talk through electronic means to some distant party, and talk about what? About nothing: "It's, like, so cool to be on the phone!"

You can make this sort of critique up about anything, pepper the essay with references to Freud, Marx, Nietzsche, Kierkegaard, and, to stay in good with conservatives, the insufferable T.S. Eliot, finish it off with a hymn to primitivism—even a wish to return to the Garden of Eden without the taint of technological sin—and you have a winning piece of commentary.

It's all nonsense.

There is plenty wrong with this genre of criticism, as Tibor Machan points out (he found someone who regretted the invention of the mirror!). But let us address the cell phone in particular, because many people seem to have bought into the idea that it represents some sort of grave danger to the culture and an ominous sign of something or other.

Of course property owners are free to ban them or not. Burger King wouldn't, but a 5-star restaurant probably would. Whatever is profitable. Private property solves whatever "problems" arise but these are not any different from other problems of what dress, speech, and behavior is right for the time and place. Certainly there is no reason to ban cell phones on flights, as the FCC is considering; leave it up to enterprise itself to decide.

The critics, however, are not satisfied. They say cell phone addiction is a broader concern. To be sure, it's easy to defend the cell phone on grounds of its emergency services. With cell phones, people have never felt more safe and secure when driving or being out and about in potentially dangerous places. The critics will concede that. What drives them nuts is casual use, the whole middle-class casual culture of the cell phone, which seems to them wholly disgusting.

And yet it is the casual use of technology that makes its emergency use ever more economically viable. It is the demand for gab that has driven up the number of providers, driven down the prices, and made amazing technologies available to all, which then provides the spillover benefit of making the emergency use of the same affordable and ubiquitous. A market of emergency-only cell service would not have become the mass phenom that it is today.

The appearance of addiction reflects a change in the use of public space made [possible] by a new technology that was born into the marketplace only in 1994. Ten years ago, talking on the phone was a

Most Used Daily Cell Phone Features: Survey of Fifteen Thousand People Worldwide

Feature	Percentage of Use
Make calls	84.60%
Use as alarm clock	82.70%
Send SMS (text messages)	78.70%
Browse the Web	78.60%
Use mobile Internet	71.20%
Use Wi-Fi	67.80%
Listen to music	60.70%
Engage in social networks	53.20%
Send/receive e-mail	51.10%
Manage your time with calendars, reminders	51.00%
Enjoy mobile games	47.70%
Look for new apps, browse apps stores	47.40%
Use the calculator	42.20%
Put down notes or tasks	40.50%
Take photos	39.00%

Taken from: GSMArena. "Mobile Phone Usage Report 2011," May 2, 2011. www.gsmarena.com.

behavior that was tied to place, namely the home or the work station. Or there was the now-anachronistic phone booth.

In retrospect, it is obvious that a vast amount of productivity was being wasted by the requirement that we be strapped to a chair, or a room in our homes, or in a glass booth, in order to keep up with work duties, friends, and family.

Suddenly and almost like magic that changed. The cell phone made it possible to speak to anyone anywhere from any place. Think of it: what a dramatic transformation. For the first time in the history of everything, anyone can have direct personal contact with anyone anytime.

No more hiding out in the home, wiling away the hours with friends, or office, which used to be all about the phone but which is now all about email and instant messaging. Professional and personal uses of phone calls can take place anywhere. We can bluetooth our way through all informal life settings and get the most out of every minute.

Not only that: it seems obvious in retrospect that audio communications are an individual and not a community affair. When the telephone first came along, you had to walk to the post office or town market to use it. What a pain. Then there were lines shared by several homes. How tedious! Then there was one phone per household—owned and maintained by the government. Please!

The ability to completely privatize audible communication had been possessed by the private sector since at least 1947 (http://www.eden.rutgers.edu/~cang/history.html), but the government hogged too much of the radio spectrum to make it possible. It wasn't until 1994 when the government deigned to provide private enterprise what it needed to create a revolution in communication.

For this reason it is useful to think of the cell phone as a freedom technology along the lines of the world wide web. It was developed by the private sector for the private sector. Both represent institutional revolts against the state's presumption to own and control the "command posts" of society. Cells and the web are the mode and means of liberation that the state will forever resent.

But back to the supposed addiction we all have. We are only making the best use of our time. What better time to talk on the phone than when other tasks are prohibited to us? You can turn driving into a multitasked operation. Same with walking to and from places. So

Fast Fact

A 2011 study published in the *Human Communication Research* journal found that smartphone users who use their devices to read the news in public settings are more likely to engage in conversation with strangers than if they were not using their phone. The authors hypothesize that the news stories provide the individuals with a topic for initiating conversation with those around them.

too with shopping at the mall. These are the very times to pull out the cell phone, not as an addiction but as a means of making the most productive use of a period of time. It is a simple matter of economizing, that is, directing resources toward their highest valued use.

But because our eyes see something new, something we haven't been socialized to expect, and because the market is expanding and democratizing so rapidly, it creates the illusion of something having gone oddly wrong. Instead of seeking to understand it, the temptation is to reach into pop culture's bag of ideological bromides and decry it as some sort of pathology.

The oddity of public phone use first dawned on the academic class several years ago when they would walk through campus and see throngs of students yammering away on the phone. Cell-phone addiction! Can these kids unplug themselves even for a minute to enjoy the scenery or talk to real people? Why should they be so very interested in their pathetic little materialist existence even after all the assigned readings from Veblen, Marx, and Derrida?

We need to realize something: these kids are walking to and from classes in which they must sit and listen and take notes for an hour or two. They are headed to another class where they will do the same. Or they might be headed to a library study session. Or they might be headed to the pool to meet friends.

In any of these cases, a phone call is not possible or desirable. But traveling from one spot to another? Shopping? Driving? It's just the time to call, even if only to leave a message.

Now, you might respond that these kids are not actually saying anything useful. They are engaged in conversational junk, punctuated by grunts of nothing. Well, productivity is a subjective concept. Meeting social obligations, making another person feel connected, letting someone know you care—these are all productive activities as understood by the individual speaking. Who are we to say what constitutes valuable or valueless conversations?

The pundit class has a penchant for judging the culture of freedom harshly. If ten years ago, these same critics had walked up and down the block peering into people's windows, they might have spied people on the phone in every home. They might have decried this as a phone addiction but nobody would have taken them seriously. In fact, the

The author asserts that people are not addicted to cell phones but are simply taking advantage of useful, easily available technology to improve their lives.

response would have been readily at hand: mind your own business, bud, and get a life.

Actually that's not a bad response to most everything that comes out of the carping class of intellectuals who try to make us feel guilty and oppressed for using products that improve our lot in life. Modern technology has us all talking to each other again. That can't be a bad thing.

EVALUATING THE AUTHOR'S ARGUMENTS:

Both viewpoint author Jeffrey A. Tucker and the *Economist* (the source of the previous viewpoint) bring up the subject of productive use of time in either supporting or condemning cell phone culture. Explain your thoughts on whether smartphones and other instant communication devices help or hinder people in making efficient or better use of their time.

Chapter 3

What Policies Can Reduce Addiction?

Whether a policy of legalizing drugs can reduce addiction has been debated for decades.

Legalization of Drugs Would Reduce Addiction

Norm Stamper

"In declaring a war on drugs, we've declared war on our fellow citizens."

The US war on drugs has cost the nation billions in enforcement and turned a large part of the population into criminals, argues Norm Stamper in the following viewpoint. Stamper, Seattle, Washington's former chief of police, claims the war must end. He favors legalizing all drugs and regulating them in a way similar to alcohol and tobacco. He believes this will help bring an end to the violence surrounding the illegal drug trade and create a new industry that will generate profits and tax revenue for the country.

AS YOU READ, CONSIDER THE FOLLOWING QUESTIONS:

1. Stamper asserts that drug abuse should not be a criminal matter but instead should be considered what kind of issue?
2. To what use does Stamper think the taxes, fees, and fines levied on legalized drugs should be put?
3. According to the author, what would happen to the national rate of drug use and abuse if drugs were legalized?

Sometimes people in law enforcement will hear it whispered that I'm a former cop who favors decriminalization of marijuana laws, and they'll approach me the way they might a traitor or snitch. So let me set the record straight.

Yes, I was a cop for 34 years, the last six of which I spent as chief of Seattle's police department.

But no, I don't favor decriminalization. I favor legalization, and not just of pot but of all drugs, including heroin, cocaine, meth, psychotropics, mushrooms and LSD.

Prohibition Does Not Work

Decriminalization, as my colleagues in the drug-reform movement hasten to inform me, takes the crime out of using drugs but continues to classify possession and use as a public offense, punishable by fines.

I've never understood why adults shouldn't enjoy the same right to use verboten drugs as they have to suck on a Marlboro or knock back a scotch and water.

Prohibition of alcohol fell flat on its face. The prohibition of other drugs rests on an equally wobbly foundation. Not until we choose to frame responsible drug use—not an oxymoron in my dictionary—as a civil liberty will we be able to recognize the abuse of drugs, including alcohol, for what it is: a medical, not a criminal, matter.

As a cop, I bore witness to the multiple lunacies of the "war on drugs." Lasting far longer than any other of our national conflicts, the drug war has been prosecuted with equal vigor by Republican and Democratic administrations, with one president after another—[Richard] Nixon, [Gerald] Ford, [Jimmy] Carter, [Ronald] Reagan, [George H.W.] Bush, [Bill] Clinton, [George W.] Bush—delivering sanctimonious sermons, squandering vast sums of taxpayer money and cheerleading law enforcers from the safety of the sidelines.

Fallout from the War on Drugs

It's not a stretch to conclude that our Draconian approach to drug use is the most injurious domestic policy since slavery. Want to cut back on prison overcrowding and save a bundle on the construction of new facilities? Open the doors, let the nonviolent drug offenders go. The huge increases in federal and state prison populations during the 1980s and '90s (from 139 per 100,000 residents in 1980 to 482 per 100,000 in 2003) were mainly for drug convictions. In 1980, 580,900 Americans were arrested on drug charges. By 2003, that figure had ballooned to 1,678,200. We're making more arrests for drug offenses than for murder, manslaughter, forcible rape and aggravated assault combined. Feel safer?

Former Seattle police chief Norm Stamper favors the legalization of all drugs because his experience has led him to believe that the war on drugs has failed.

I've witnessed the devastating effects of open-air drug markets in residential neighborhoods: children recruited as runners, mules and lookouts; drug dealers and innocent citizens shot dead in firefights between rival traffickers bent on protecting or expanding their markets; dedicated narcotics officers tortured and killed in the line of duty; prisons filled with nonviolent drug offenders; and drug-related foreign policies that foster political instability, wreak health and environmental disasters, and make life even tougher for indigenous subsistence farmers in places such as Latin America and Afghanistan. All because we like our drugs—and can't have them without breaking the law.

As an illicit commodity, drugs cost and generate extravagant sums of (laundered, untaxed) money, a powerful magnet for character-challenged police officers.

Although small in numbers of offenders, there isn't a major police force—the Los Angeles [California] Police Department included—that has escaped the problem: cops, sworn to uphold the law, seizing

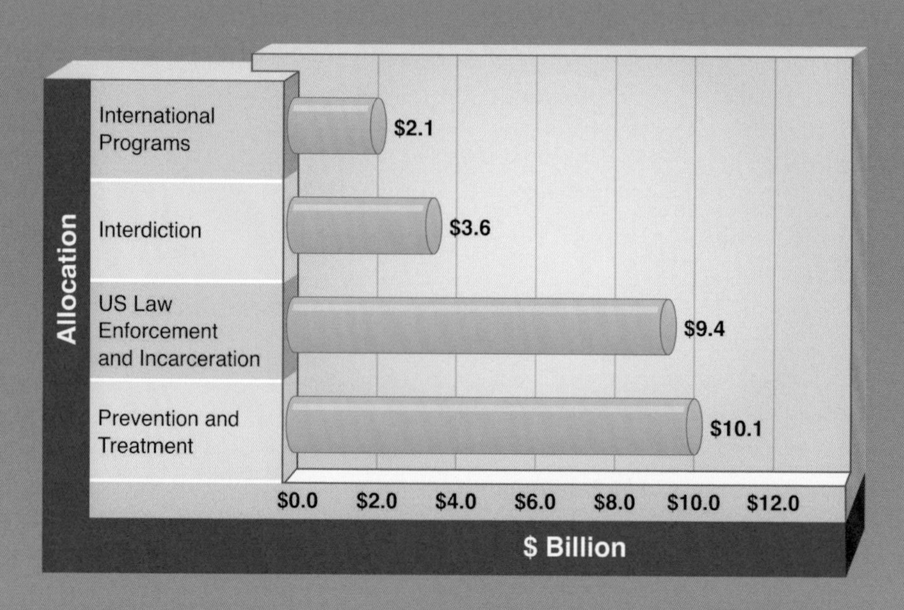

Taken from: Office of National Drug Control Policy. *2012 National Drug Control Strategy.* Washington, DC: ONDCP, 2012.

and converting drugs to their own use, planting dope on suspects, robbing and extorting pushers, taking up dealing themselves, intimidating or murdering witnesses.

Making Citizens into Enemies

In declaring a war on drugs, we've declared war on our fellow citizens. War requires "hostiles"—enemies we can demonize, fear and loathe. This unfortunate categorization of millions of our citizens justifies treating them as dope fiends, less than human. That grants political license to ban the exchange or purchase of clean needles or to withhold methadone from heroin addicts motivated to kick the addiction.

President [George W.] Bush has even said no to medical marijuana. Why would he want to "coddle" the enemy? Even if the enemy is a suffering AIDS or cancer patient for whom marijuana promises palliative, if not therapeutic, powers.

> **FAST FACT**
>
> **In 2001 Portugal implemented a national policy that decriminalized the use of all drugs and instituted a policy of treatment instead of incarceration for drug users. Ten years later Portuguese health experts and government officials reported that the number of addicts had been reduced by 60 percent.**

As a nation, we're long overdue for a soul-searching, coldly analytical look at both the "drug scene" and the drug war. Such candor would reveal the futility of our current policies, exposing the embarrassingly meager return on our massive enforcement investment (about $69 billion a year, according to Jack Cole, founder and executive director of Law Enforcement Against Prohibition).

How would "regulated legalization" work? It would:

- Permit private companies to compete for licenses to cultivate, harvest, manufacture, package and peddle drugs.
- Create a new federal regulatory agency (with no apologies to libertarians or paleo-conservatives).
- Set and enforce standards of sanitation, potency and purity.
- Ban advertising.

- Impose (with congressional approval) taxes, fees and fines to be used for drug-abuse prevention and treatment and to cover the costs of administering the new regulatory agency.
- Police the industry much as alcoholic-beverage-control agencies keep a watch on bars and liquor stores at the state level. Such reforms would in no way excuse drug users who commit crimes: driving while impaired, providing drugs to minors, stealing an iPod, assaulting one's spouse, abusing one's child. The message is simple. Get loaded, commit a crime, do the time.

Expected Results of Legalization

These reforms would yield major reductions in a host of predatory street crimes, a disproportionate number of which are committed by users who resort to stealing in order to support their addiction.

Regulated legalization would soon dry up most stockpiles of currently illicit drugs—substances of uneven, often questionable quality (including "bunk," i.e., fakes such as oregano, gypsum, baking powder or even poisons passed off as the genuine article). It would extract from today's drug dealing the obscene profits that attract the needy and the greedy and fuel armed violence. And it would put most of those certifiably frightening crystal meth labs out of business once and for all.

Combined with treatment, education and other public-health programs for drug abusers, regulated legalization would make your city or town an infinitely healthier place to live and raise a family.

It would make being a cop a much safer occupation, and it would lead to greater police accountability and improved morale and job satisfaction.

But wouldn't regulated legalization lead to more users and, more to the point, drug abusers? Probably, though no one knows for sure—our leaders are too timid even to broach the subject in polite circles, much less to experiment with new policy models. My own prediction? We'd see modest increases in use, negligible increases in abuse.

The demand for illicit drugs is as strong as the nation's thirst for bootleg booze during Prohibition. It's a demand that simply will not dry up. Whether to find God, heighten sex, relieve pain, drown one's sorrows or simply feel good, people throughout the millenniums have turned to mood- and mind-altering substances.

They're not about to stop, no matter what their government says or does. It's time to accept drug use as a right of adult Americans, treat drug abuse as a public-health problem and end the madness of an unwinnable war.

EVALUATING THE AUTHOR'S ARGUMENTS:

Norm Stamper is a former police official who argues that legalization of drugs would make communities safer and reduce addiction. Do you find his evidence convincing? Why or why not?

Viewpoint

2

Legalization of Drugs Would Increase Addiction

"There is **no** *reason to think today's levels* **of** *addiction are anywhere near the levels that would be reached under legalization."*

George F. Will

George F. Will, a veteran political and domestic affairs columnist for the *Washington Post*, responds in the following viewpoint to calls for the legalization of drugs in the United States. According to Will, critics suggest that America should try legalization in order to end ballooning enforcement and incarceration costs, but he insists the experiment would likely have negative consequences. Primarily, Will believes that legitimizing drugs would create new users who previously would have been scared off by their illicit nature. He fears that more users would result in another public health crisis comparable to the ones associated with alcohol and tobacco use. For this and other reasons, Will is skeptical of legalization as a solution to the nation's drug problem.

AS YOU READ, CONSIDER THE FOLLOWING QUESTIONS:

1. How many Americans are incarcerated for dealing drugs, according to Will?
2. What drug does the author say kills more people than alcohol and illicit drugs combined?
3. What does Will think would happen if the nation tried to use taxes to inflate cocaine and heroin prices to keep the number of users under control?

The human nervous system interacts in pleasing and addictive ways with certain molecules derived from some plants, which is why humans may have developed beer before they developed bread. Psychoactive—consciousness-altering—and addictive drugs are natural, a fact that should immunize policymakers against extravagant hopes as they cope with America's drug problem, which is convulsing some nations to our south.

The costs—human, financial and social—of combating (most) drugs are prompting calls for decriminalization or legalization. America should, however, learn from the psychoactive drug used by a majority of American adults—alcohol.

Mark Kleiman of UCLA [University of California, Los Angeles], a policy analyst, was recently discussing drug policy with someone who said he had no experience with illegal drugs, not even marijuana, because he is of "the gin generation." Ah, said Kleiman, gin: "A much more dangerous drug." Twenty percent of all American prisoners—500,000 people—are incarcerated for dealing illegal drugs, but alcohol causes as much as half of America's criminal violence and vehicular fatalities.

The Costs of Already Legalized Substances

Drinking alcohol had been a widely exercised private right for millennia when America tried to prohibit it. As a public-health measure, Prohibition "worked": Alcohol-related illnesses declined dramatically. As the monetary cost of drinking tripled, deaths from cirrhosis of the liver declined by a third. This improvement was, however, paid for in the coin of rampant criminality and disrespect for law.

Prohibition resembled what is today called decriminalization: It did not make drinking illegal; it criminalized the making, importing, transporting or selling of alcohol. Drinking remained legal, so oceans of it were made, imported, transported and sold.

Another legal drug, nicotine, kills more people than do alcohol and all illegal drugs—combined. For decades, government has aggressively publicized the health risks of smoking and made it unfashionable, stigmatized, expensive and inconvenient. Yet 20 percent of every rising American generation becomes addicted to nicotine.

Fast Fact

The US Drug Enforcement Administration reports that following the relaxation of drug laws in Netherlands, which allowed the public sale of marijuana, use of this drug by eighteen- to twenty-five-year-olds doubled, and heroin addiction tripled.

So, suppose cocaine or heroin were legalized and marketed as cigarettes and alcohol are. And suppose the level of addiction were to replicate the 7 percent of adults suffering from alcohol abuse or dependency. That would be a public health disaster. As the late James Q. Wilson said, nicotine shortens life, cocaine debases it.

Creating More Demand and More Supply

Still, because the costs of prohibition—interdiction, mass incarceration, etc.—are staggeringly high, some people say, "Let's just try legalization for a while." Society is not, however, like a controlled laboratory; in society, experiments that produce disappointing or unexpected results cannot be tidily reversed.

Legalized marijuana could be produced for much less than a tenth of its current price as an illegal commodity. Legalization of cocaine and heroin would cut their prices, too; they would sell for a tiny percentage of their current prices. And using high excise taxes to maintain cocaine and heroin prices at current levels would produce widespread tax evasion—and an illegal market.

Furthermore, legalization would mean drugs of reliable quality would be conveniently available from clean stores for customers not

George F. Will believes that legalizing drugs would create many new users who would have not taken drugs if they were still illegal.

risking the stigma of breaking the law in furtive transactions with unsavory people. So there is *no* reason to think today's levels of addiction are anywhere near the levels that would be reached under legalization.

Regarding the interdicting of drug shipments, capturing "kingpin" distributors and incarcerating dealers, consider data from the

Types of Illicit Drug Use in the Past Year Among Persons Aged Twelve or Older: Percentages, 2002–2010

Drug	Year								
	2002	2003	2004	2005	2006	2007	2008	2009	2010
Illicit drugs	**14.9**	**14.7**	**14.5**	**14.4**	**14.5**	**14.4**	**14.2**	**15.1**	**15.3**
Marijuana and hashish	11.0	10.6	10.6	10.4	10.3	10.1	10.3	11.3	11.5
Cocaine	2.5	2.5	2.4	2.3	2.5	2.3	2.1	1.9	1.8
Crack	0.7	0.6	0.5	0.6	0.6	0.6	0.4	0.4	0.3
Heroin	0.2	0.1	0.2	0.2	0.2	0.1	0.2	0.2	0.2
Hallucinogens	2.0	1.7	1.6	1.6	1.6	1.5	1.5	1.8	1.8
LSD	0.4	0.2	0.2	0.2	0.3	0.3	0.3	0.3	0.3
PCP	0.1	0.1	0.1	0.1	0.1	0.1	0.0	0.0	0.0
Ecstasy	1.3	0.9	0.8	0.8	0.9	0.9	0.9	1.1	1.0
Inhalants	0.9	0.9	0.9	0.9	0.9	0.8	0.8	0.8	0.8
Nonmedical use of psychotherapeutics	6.3	6.4	6.2	6.3	6.7	6.6	6.1	6.4	6.3
Pain relievers	4.7	4.9	4.7	4.9	5.1	5.0	4.8	4.9	4.8
OxyContin®	–	–	0.5	0.5	0.5	0.6	0.6	0.7	0.7
Tranquilizers	2.1	2.1	2.1	2.2	2.1	2.1	2.0	2.2	2.2
Stimulants	1.4	1.3	1.4	1.3	1.5	1.2	1.1	1.2	1.1
Methamphetamine	0.7	0.7	0.8	0.7	0.8	0.5	0.3	0.5	0.4
Sedatives	0.4	0.3	0.3	0.3	0.4	0.3	0.2	0.3	0.4
Illicit drugs other than marijuana	**8.7**	**8.5**	**8.2**	**8.3**	**8.6**	**8.5**	**8.0**	**8.3**	**8.1**

Taken from: Substance Abuse and Mental Health Services Administration. *2010 National Survey on Drug Use & Health*. Rockville, MD: SAMHSA, 2011.

book "Drugs and Drug Policy: What Everyone Needs to Know" by Kleiman, Jonathan Caulkins and Angela Hawken. Almost all heroin comes from poppies grown on 4 percent of the arable land of one country—Afghanistan. Four South American countries—Colombia, Ecuador, Peru and Bolivia—produce more than 90 percent of the world's cocaine. But attempts to decrease production in source countries produce the "balloon effect." Squeeze a balloon in one spot, it bulges in another. Suppress production of poppies or coca leaves here, production moves there. The $8 billion Plan Colombia [US legislation aimed at reducing drug smuggling] was a melancholy success, reducing coca production there 65 percent, while production increased 40 percent in Peru and doubled in Bolivia.

In the 1980s, when "cocaine cowboys" made Miami lawless, the U.S. government created the South Florida Task Force to interdict cocaine shipped from Central and South America by small planes and cigarette boats. This interdiction was so successful the cartels opened new delivery routes. Tranquility in Miami was purchased at the price of mayhem in Mexico.

America spends 20 times more on drug control than all the world's poppy and coca growers earn.

EVALUATING THE AUTHOR'S ARGUMENTS:

Viewpoint author George F. Will contends that the problems associated with tobacco and alcohol use should convince Americans that legalization of drugs would create more addicts and bring about another health crisis. Do you believe Will's argument is sound, or is there reason to believe that legalization would not lead to more social costs than are currently accrued under the war on drugs? Explain your answer.

Legalized Internet Gambling Would Lead to Increases in Pathological Gambling

"The results of legalization [of online gambling] . . . offers few advantages to the economy or tax base but incredible pain to families across the country."

Spencer Bachus

In the following viewpoint Spencer Bachus applauds the Unlawful Internet Gambling Enforcement Act of 2006 as an effective means of curbing Internet gambling. According to Bachus, Internet gambling is run by offshore corporations that prey on players who fail to recognize the dangers of betting with credit cards and "virtual" money. He claims that too many players become addicts, leading to huge debts or bankruptcy. Bachus is thankful that many officials at the federal and state levels support continued prohibition of Internet gambling, resisting lobbyists who call for legalization. Serving the state of Alabama, Bachus is a Republican member of the US House of Representatives.

Spencer Bachus, "Should Online Gambling Be Legalized? No," *US News Digital Weekly*, May 22, 2009.

AS YOU READ, CONSIDER THE FOLLOWING QUESTIONS:

1. Why does Bachus claim that young people are especially vulnerable to the temptation of Internet gambling?
2. According to the author, what did Greg Hogan's son do in an attempt to pay off debts accumulated from his Internet gambling addiction?
3. As Bachus estimates, how much money were offshore Internet gambling sites raking in before the passage of the 2006 law?

Proponents of legalizing online gambling call prohibitions a sucker's bet—sacrificing freedom to gain the moral high ground but little else. Opponents cite states' rights and problem gambling, as well as a need to protect young citizens from vices. Should online betting be legal?

In the history of our country, the federal government has never authorized or sanctioned gambling of any kind. Now, offshore casino interests are leading an unprecedented effort to legalize Internet gambling.

Internet gambling's characteristics are unique: Online players can gamble 24 hours a day, seven days a week from home; children may play without sufficient age verification; and betting with a credit card can undercut a player's perception of the value of cash, leading to addiction, bankruptcy, and crime. Young people are particularly at risk because a computer in the bedroom or dorm room of a young person is a temptation that many may fall prey to.

An Effective Government Policy

For more than a decade, Congress has sought to deter, not promote, Internet gambling. It has always been illegal, but until recently no one could enforce the law because the casinos were offshore, far away from the jurisdiction of law enforcement.

The bipartisan passage of the Unlawful Internet Gambling Enforcement Act [UIGEA] in 2006 has helped end this shell game. The federal government was given new tools to enforce old rules prohibiting online gambling contained in statutes like the Wire Act of 1961. The 2006 law was designed to make it impossible to use a bank instrument like a credit card or money transfer or check to settle an illegal online wager.

Even though opponents have delayed and tried to block implementation, UIGEA is already working. According to an Annenberg Public Policy Center survey, after enactment of the law, weekly use of the Internet for gambling among college-age youth fell from 5.8 percent to 1.5 percent from 2006 to 2007. A November 2008 follow-up by the center stated, "The strong drop in weekly use of Internet sites following [its] passage appears to remain in place."

Unfortunately, this came too late for Greg Hogan's family in Hudson, Ohio. He described to our Financial Services Committee how his son, the president of his class at Lehigh University, became a gambling addict. Realizing the problem, Hogan installed protective software on his son's computer to prevent him from gambling online. But offshore casinos can find ways to bypass these filters, and the young man accumulated such massive gambling debts that he robbed a bank to try to pay them off. He was sent to prison.

Concerned about the integrity of their games, professional and college sports organizations urged passage of the antigambling law. Major League Baseball, the NFL [National Football League], the NBA [National Basketball Association], the NHL [National Hockey League], and the NCAA [National Collegiate Athletic Association] have sent numerous letters to Congress supporting the law, most recently on May 14, 2009. University presidents have shared concerns about the integrity of the athletic competitions on their fields and about students betting in their dorm rooms.

States Support the Ban

Our country has a long tradition of allowing the states to regulate gambling and not permitting the federal government to override decisions made by the states and their citizens. In this particular case, the federal government would be overturning laws in 50 states that regulate gambling. The state attorneys general say they need the antigambling law. Without it, they have no effective way to combat illegal Internet gambling occurring in their jurisdictions.

Recognizing the importance of the law, Attorney General Eric Holder promised to vigorously enforce it when asked about it during his Senate confirmation hearing. Aside from the Department of Justice, the State Department has testified, "The Internet gambling operations are, in essence, the functional equivalent of wholly unregulated offshore banks with the bettor accounts serving as bank accounts for account holders who are, in the virtual world, virtually anonymous. For these reasons, Internet gambling operations are vulnerable to be used not only for money laundering but also for criminal activities ranging from terrorist financing to tax evasion."

A Predatory Industry Ready to Pounce

Supporters of legalization argue that prohibition has sent Internet gambling underground and left the vulnerable unprotected. But it was the 2006 law that finally safeguarded families from predatory intrusion into their homes. The alternatives—age verification and geographic location softwares—are simply ineffective and easy to elude.

Before 2006, offshore Internet casinos were proliferating, raking in more than $6 billion illegally from Americans every year. One can understand why they are spending millions of dollars on lobbyists to try to get back in the game. But if Congress repeals this widely supported law, online casinos will become ubiquitous. One company has even developed gambling software for iPhones that will be on the market the day online gambling is legalized by the federal government.

Fast Fact

In October 2011 Keith S. Whyte, the executive director of the National Council on Problem Gambling, testified before the US House of Representatives that half a million teens (aged twelve to seventeen) in the United States have a gambling addiction based on the diagnostic criteria, making gambling addiction a problem as serious as prescription drug abuse.

It took places like Las Vegas [Nevada] and Atlantic City [New Jersey] years to develop effective gambling regulations, and they have had decades of experience enforcing them. Yet this new legislation would direct the Treasury Department to set up a new regulatory regime to oversee shadowy foreign gaming enterprises in a mere matter of months.

Even if one concedes that legalization and regulation could possibly prevent underage gambling, compulsive play, cheating by casinos as documented by *60 Minutes* and the *Washington Post*, and money laundering or drug trafficking by criminals on U.S.-sanctioned gambling sites, the pre-2006 problem of predatory, illegal offshore casino bets would return. One country's rules would be woefully insufficient. Ultimately, the results of legalization would be expanding, sanctioning, and inevitably losing control of an industry that offers few advantages to the economy or tax base but incredible pain to families across the country.

It's a gamble that simply is not worth taking.

EVALUATING THE AUTHOR'S ARGUMENTS:

How does Spencer Bachus illustrate his claim that Internet gambling has widespread opposition in the United States? Does his list of detractors persuade you that this industry needs to be curbed? Why or why not?

Legalized Internet Gambling Would Not Lead to Increases in Pathological Gambling

"Legalization of online poker would actually improve efforts to assist pathological gamblers."

Frank J. Fahrenkopf Jr.

Frank J. Fahrenkopf Jr. is a lawyer and president of the American Gaming Association, an advocacy group for the gambling industry. In the following viewpoint, he maintains that online poker is a popular form of gambling that will continue to attract American players despite its current illegal status. Fahrenkopf argues that online poker should be licensed and regulated so that the industry can be monitored and made safe. In addition, Fahrenkopf claims that regulation will allow the industry to track problem gamblers and help individuals set limits

Frank J. Fahrenkopf Jr.,"Testimony Submitted for Consideration by the US House Committee on Energy and Commerce Subcommitte on Commerce, Manufacturing, and Trade," Congressional Testimony, October 24, 2011.

on losses. Fahrenkopf maintains that studies show that permitting online gambling does not lead to more abuse and addiction, but he insists that legalizing online poker will implement safeguards that will inhibit problem gambling and promote responsible play.

AS YOU READ, CONSIDER THE FOLLOWING QUESTIONS:

1. Why does Fahrenkopf claim that online poker is substantially different from other forms of Internet gambling?
2. What types of technology does Fahrenkopf say will help players manage their online gambling in real time?
3. What percentage of the US adult population are pathological gamblers, according to the author?

For much of the time since Internet gambling was first introduced, the AGA [American Gaming Association] urged caution as the country considered the legalization of Internet gambling. We simply were not convinced that Internet gambling could be regulated to protect Americans against fraud, money laundering and other illegal activities. We also were concerned that Internet gambling companies wouldn't be able to prevent minors from gambling on their sites and that there weren't sufficient safeguards to protect problem gamblers.

New technology and new processes have changed that. We live in a digital world where people can purchase everything from groceries to automobiles online. These e-commerce companies have developed new technology and processes to help them facilitate sales, protect customers and, in some cases, prevent minors from purchasing their products. The same types of technological and process advancements are being used in countries such as Great Britain, France, and Italy and in provinces of Canada to effectively regulate and oversee Internet gambling. Those countries and others have proven that the technology and processes exist to effectively eliminate the risks that contributed to the passage of the Unlawful Internet Gaming Enforcement Act (UIGEA).

Because of the technological and process advancements now available to the gaming industry, we now support the right of states to license online poker, should they choose to do so, through the passage of legislation that would strengthen and enhance UIGEA and provide a strong regulatory framework for states to follow.

Support for Online Poker

You might ask, "Why just online poker?" Poker is substantially different than other forms of gaming. First, it is a game that vast numbers of Americans have historically played and that millions of Americans still play. In fact, the jargon of poker is woven throughout our language with phrases such as blue chip, pass the buck, high roller, wild card, poker face and up the ante.

Second, unlike other forms of Internet gambling, poker is primarily a game of skill. And, poker is played between or among individuals, whereas in other forms of Internet gambling the customer is playing against the "house." Finally, the support we've seen around the country is really focused on online poker and not on other forms of Internet gambling.

The fact is practically every adult in the country has played poker at one time or another, and today the preferred venue for millions of poker players is the Internet.

Last year [in 2010], in the United States, an estimated 10 million to 15 million people bet billions of dollars online, even though it is illegal for companies to offer real-money Internet gambling in the U.S. Americans will continue to bet online as long as there are sites they can access, and we can expect that there will always be sites they can access as long as there are billions of dollars to be made.

Regulation Trumps Outlawing

While we applaud the efforts of law enforcement agencies to crack down on illegal off shore gambling sites, they can only make temporary gains. For example, following enactment of the UIGEA in 2006, several major offshore operators stopped taking bets from U.S. residents, and for a period of time the volume of online betting from the U.S. decreased.

Yet the market recovered with new sites coming online, and in 2010, Internet gambling revenues from U.S. bettors exceeded $4 billion.

Even the indictments of executives from several online poker companies last April [2011] did not stop Internet gambling. In fact, in the immediate aftermath of online poker's "Black Friday," the companies that continue to operate in the U.S. saw a surge in new business. Shortly after that event, it was estimated there were still more than 1,000 real-money websites operated by nearly 300 offshore operators targeting the U.S. market. This is further proof that offshore operators will continue to cater to demand and develop new techniques to circumvent the barriers we put in place. The volume may fluctuate with each closed website and set of indictments, but demand will prevail in the end.

Fast Fact

An international study by Ingo Fiedler of the University of Hamburg found that of the approximately 6 million individuals playing online poker worldwide, 22 percent spent less than one hour playing, 28 percent spent 1 to 5 hours, 20 percent spent 5 to 15 hours, 13 percent spent 15 to 35 hours, 11 percent spent 35 to 100 hours, and only 6 percent spent more than 100 hours over a six-month period.

Moreover, it is very likely that Internet gambling operators who fill this void will be even less regulated and less trustworthy than their predecessors, which will only hurt American consumers.

Put simply, the current environment puts American online players at risk. It is practically impossible to ensure that children are not gambling online and that the Internet gambling companies are acting responsibly towards those who cannot gamble responsibly. These companies, by illegally operating in the U.S., are flouting our laws; they are doing it where law enforcement cannot reach them and where, in many cases, there is little to no regulatory oversight. . . .

Consumers could be saved from this risk if UIGEA were strengthened so states that wanted to could license and regulate online poker, following federal guidelines. We know U.S.-licensed gaming companies, following time-tested gaming regulations, would provide safe, honest, responsible sites for the use of the men and women who want to play online poker. A strengthened UIGEA also would protect Americans from unscrupulous operators and would have the added advantage of bringing the jobs and revenues associated with this billion-dollar industry back to the United States. . . .

Monitoring Play

Preventing cheating, whether by humans or software programs, is made easy through the use of fraud and collusion monitoring technology, coupled with reporting of suspicious play by other players.

And, efforts to launder money are detected through a number of reports and checks used exclusively by the gaming industry, as well as other processes that are common in financial institutions. Among those processes are spotting unusual deposit and cash-out patterns, and identifying players who frequently play with the same players or frequently lose to the same players. Other safeguards include having processes that don't allow a person-to-person transfer of funds because operational controls ensure that money deposited with an online poker company would always return to its original source.

The author claims that online poker games can be adequately controlled to avoid players' becoming addicted or going too far into debt.

Technology also allows players to manage their gambling in real time by doing things such as designating a set amount of money or time they can spend on the site, asking for a cooling off period and, if they feel they have lost control of their gambling, choosing to self-exclude.

With these processes and the technology that supports them in place, patrons could play poker online in a safe, honest place. Law enforcement would be helped by operators' ability to quickly identify possible fraud and other criminal activities. And, the public could be confident that operators are taking bets only from jurisdictions where it is legal, keeping minors from gambling and providing assistance to problem gamblers. . . .

American Gaming Association Poll Concerning Compulsive Gambling

"Who should take the most responsibility for addressing the problem of compulsive gambling in the United States today?"

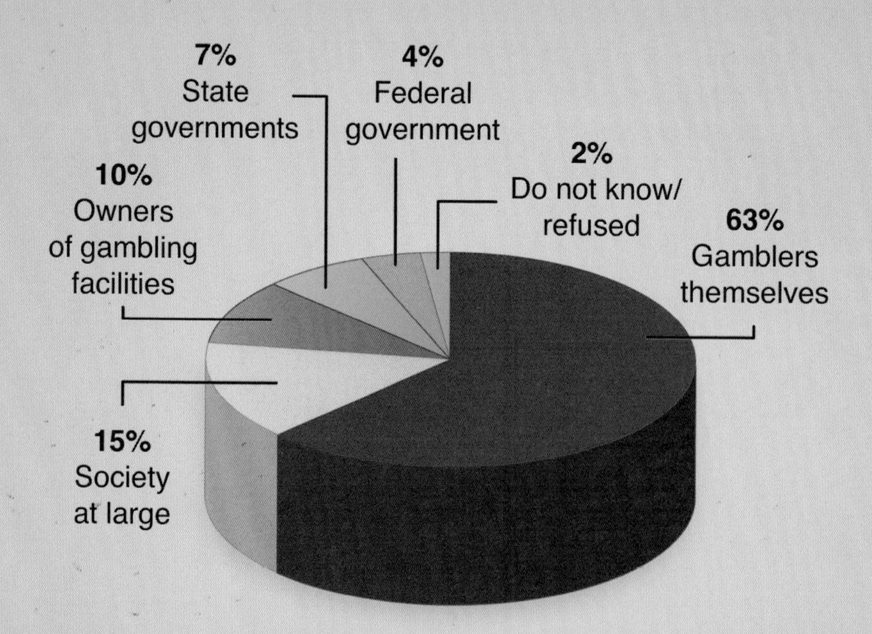

Taken from: Ben Harper and Beth Lawton. "Gambling Addictions Increasing, but Help Is Not." Medill News Service, 2003.

No Increase in Problem Gambling

I would like to take the opportunity to address in more detail the question of the impact of online poker on problem gambling.

It is settled science that at any given time that about 1 percent of the U.S. adult population are pathological gamblers. Researchers also have found no evidence that Internet gamblers are more likely to be pathological gamblers. In fact, a major British study found no increase in the rate of pathological gambling between 1999 and 2007, even though Internet gambling became widely available during that period. Similar results emerged in a study of Swedish gamblers.

More recently, in a 2010 article in *Addiction Research and Theory*, Dr. Howard J. Shaffer, director of the Division on Addictions and associate professor of psychiatry at Harvard Medical School, and his colleagues offered a comprehensive look at the research conducted to date, including summaries of their own investigations of the gambling patterns of customers of bwin.party, one of Europe's largest Internet gambling companies.

Professor Shaffer and his colleagues have pioneered new methods for studying Internet gambling by virtue of their access to the actual wagering transactions of 40,000 online gamblers, including every keystroke of every person who subscribes to the bwin.party website. These data, which reflect *actual* gambling patterns rather than relying on self-reporting, provide "objective detailed information about betting behavior and the conditions under which gamblers place wagers."

The analysis of the bwin.party data has produced seven peer-reviewed publications that contradict the notion that Internet gambling breeds excessive and problematic gambling Although the prevalence of pathological gambling is low, and even though there is no evidence that Internet gambling would change that pattern, it is still important that online poker companies should implement responsible gaming programs just as brick-and-mortar casinos do.

By requiring licensed websites to include social responsibility protections, legalization of online poker would actually improve efforts to assist pathological gamblers. Today, without any U.S. regulation, there are no uniform requirements for player protection tools at gambling websites. Indeed, many foreign jurisdictions require no such tools, so gambling operators located in those jurisdictions often do not provide them. For these reasons, the report by Shaffer et al. concluded that "regulators should be able to design sufficient protections to prevent any significant growth in problem gambling that results from legalization."

In conclusion, the safe bet is to allow states to license and regulate online poker following federal guidelines. Such action would protect U.S. consumers, keep children from gambling on the Internet, and provide the tools law enforcement needs to shut down illegal Internet gambling operators. It would also create new jobs and tax revenue at a time when both are sorely needed.

EVALUATING THE AUTHOR'S ARGUMENTS:

Frank J. Fahrenkopf Jr. is a member of a gaming industry advocacy organization. Does that fact affect your opinion of the evidence he gives in his viewpoint? Why or why not, and if so, how?

Facts About Addiction

Editor's note: These facts can be used in reports to add credibility when making important points or claims.

Tobacco Addiction

In 2010, 45.3 million adults, or 19.3 percent of the total adult population, in the United States were smokers according to the Centers for Disease Control and Prevention (CDC). This is almost one out of every five adults.

The CDC conducted a survey in 2009 that found more than one out of four high school students used tobacco (whether by smoking or using smokeless tobacco), and close to half of the students surveyed had tried smoking cigarettes at some point.

Approximately 440,000 people in the United States die from diseases linked to tobacco use every year, according to a 2008 CDC *Morbidity and Mortality Weekly Report.*

According to the 2007 National Center on Addiction and Substance Abuse at Columbia University (CASAColumbia) report "Tobacco: The Smoking Gun," teens aged twelve to seventeen who smoke cigarettes are five times as likely to drink and thirteen times as likely to use marijuana than those who do not smoke.

Alcohol Addiction

The 2010 National Survey on Drug Use and Health (NSDUH) found that 51.8 percent of the US population over the age of twelve consider themselves to be current drinkers.

The 2010 NSDUH found that 16.9 million people in the United States above the age of twelve reported that they are heavy drinkers.

Around 40 percent of individuals who start drinking alcohol before the age of fifteen become alcoholics, according to the National Institute on Drug Abuse (NIDA) in its April 2011 revision of the publication "Drugs: Shatter the Myths."

The NIDA's 2011 "Drugs: Shatter the Myths" reports that each year underage drinking results in the death of around five thousand individuals under the age of twenty-one; of that total, almost 40 percent die from injuries sustained in car crashes.

Marijuana Addiction

The 2009 NSDUH found that 16.7 million Americans who were at least twelve years old used marijuana at least once in the month before the survey.

The NIDA's 2011 Monitoring the Future Survey found that 6.6 percent of high school seniors use marijuana every day.

The November 2010 NIDA fact sheet on marijuana reports that approximately 9 percent of people who use marijuana become addicted.

The NIDA stated in November 2010 that 17 percent of individuals seeking addiction treatment in 2008 were admitted for marijuana addiction.

Addiction to Prescription Drugs

According to the 2010 NSDUH, approximately 2.4 million Americans used prescription drugs for nonmedical purposes.

The 2010 NSDUH found that 5.9 percent of young adults from 18 to 25 years of age admitted to using prescription medication nonmedically, and 3 percent of adolescents aged 12 to 17 admitted to using them nonmedically.

The 2010 NSDUH found that after alcohol, marijuana, and tobacco, prescription and over-the-counter drugs are the most commonly abused substances among twelfth graders.

A 2011 study by the CDC found that opioid pain relievers (such as Vicodin and OxyContin) accounted for more deaths in every age group of users than illegal drugs (such as cocaine and heroin).

Gambling Addiction

According to undated information from the National Council on Problem Gambling, under current diagnostic criteria, in a given year, approximately 2 million adults in the United States can be considered pathological gamblers; 4 million–6 million additional adults would be considered problem gamblers because they meet only one or more, but not all, of the diagnostic criteria.

A June 2008 article titled "The Prevalence of Problem Gambling Among US Adolescents and Young Adults: Results from a National Survey," published in the *Journal of Gambling Studies,* found that 2.1 percent of youth aged fourteen to twenty-one could be considered problem gamblers.

The annual social cost of gambling-related addiction, bankruptcy, and crime can be estimated at $7 billion, according to the 2012 National Problem Gambling Awareness Week website.

Addiction Treatment

According to the 2007 NSDUH, of the estimated 23.2 million people in the United States who needed treatment for use of an illicit drug or alcohol abuse, only 2.4 million received treatment at a facility such as a hospital, rehab center, or mental health center.

The NIDA September 2009 fact sheet on treatment options for drug addiction states that medications can be used to aid an individual who is going through withdrawal after drug use is stopped; medications can also help to reduce the incidence of relapse by making cravings less intense.

Organizations to Contact

The editors have compiled the following list of organizations concerned with the issues debated in this book. The descriptions are derived from materials provided by the organizations. All have publications or information available for interested readers. The list was compiled on the date of publication of the present volume; the information provided here may change. Be aware that many organizations take several weeks or longer to respond to inquiries, so allow as much time as possible for the receipt of requested materials.

Alcoholics Anonymous (AA)
PO Box 459
New York, NY 10163
(212) 870-3400
website: www.aa.org

AA is a group of individuals that support each other as they work to address the problems they have all faced as a result of their alcoholism and take steps to recover and maintain sobriety. The organization employs a 12-step program for recovery, and individuals can attend local meetings and work with sponsors to quit using alcohol. Detailed information about AA and how to become a member can be found on the organization's website along with AA books, pamphlets, and newsletters.

American Psychological Association (APA)
750 First St. NE
Washington, DC 20002-4242
(202) 336-5500; toll-free: (800) 374-2721
website: www.apa.org

The APA is the national professional organization of psychologists in the United States, with a membership comprising more than 137,000 researchers, educators, clinicians, consultants, and students. The association seeks to advance the field of psychology as a means of improving both society and the lives of individuals. The APA researches all types of addiction and publishes reports and findings on its website; examples of reports include "Developing Medications to Treat Addiction: Challenges for Science, Policy, and Practice," "Drug Abuse & Addiction," and "The Genetics of Drug Abuse and Addiction."

American Society of Addiction Medicine (ASAM)
4601 N. Park Ave., Upper Arcade, Ste. 101,
Chevy Chase, MD 20815-4520
(301) 656-3920
fax: (301) 656-3815
e-mail: email@asam.org
website: www.asam.org

ASAM is a professional society of physicians seeking to advance the role of medical care in addiction treatment through increased access and improved quality of treatment, education, and research. The organization promotes the belief that addiction is a medical disease and must be treated accordingly with medication and physician assistance. Published quarterly, the *Journal of Addiction Medicine* is the official publication of the ASAM, and articles in the journal cover all types of addiction, from drugs to alcohol to gambling. Additional articles and resources can be accessed on the ASAM website.

Centers for Disease Control and Prevention (CDC)
1600 Clifton Rd.
Atlanta, GA 30333
(800) 232-4636
e-mail: cdcinfo@cdc.gov
website: www.cdc.gov

The CDC is the government department charged with protecting the health of US citizens, preventing disease, and preparing for new health threats. As one facet of this mission, the CDC investigates addiction to tobacco, alcohol, and other drugs. It conducts surveys to assess the levels of addiction in the population and carries out research to determine strategies for prevention and treatment. Extensive data and reports can be found on the CDC website, including "National Drug Control Strategy, 2009 Annual Report," and "Drugs, Brains and Behavior—the Science of Addiction."

Drug Policy Alliance (DPA)
Office of National Affairs, 925 Fifteenth St. NW, 2nd Fl.
Washington, DC 20005
(202) 216-0035
fax: (202) 216-0803
e-mail: dc@drugpolicy.org
website: www.drugpolicy.org

DPA promotes alternative options for combating drug use and its accompanying problems in the United States. The organization opposes the war on drugs and seeks to advance policy based on scientific research, compassion, health, and human rights. Some of the main issues tackled by DPA include reforming marijuana laws, fighting injustice, reducing drug harm, and protecting youth. Articles detailing the importance of these topics, as well as the action being taken by the organization, can be read on the DPA website.

Food Addiction Institute (FAI)
(941) 474-1972
e-mail: info@foodaddictioninstitute.org
website: www.foodaddictioninstitute.org

The FAI has been working since 2005 to find new ways to tackle the problem of food addiction that is a part of the larger obesity epidemic. In that time, the organization has published numerous books and articles detailing food addiction, standardized a training program for food addiction professionals, and helped found new recovery facilities for food addicts. The organization is currently working to expand its reach and increase awareness about food addiction and options for recovery. On the FAI website visitors can find detailed definitions of food addiction and read reports such as "Physical Craving and Food Addiction: A Scientific Review."

Food and Drug Administration (FDA)
10903 New Hampshire Ave.
Silver Spring, MD 20993
(888) INFO-FDA (463-6332)
website: www.fda.gov

The FDA is a US government agency that is part of the US Department of Health and Human Services. The administration's main duties are ensuring that human and veterinary drugs, medical devices, the food supply, cosmetics, and dietary supplements all meet standards of safety, effectiveness, and quality. The FDA also oversees the regulation of tobacco products. With regard to tobacco, the agency provides guidelines on acceptable marketing and labeling and makes sure that all tobacco companies comply with these and other guidelines. The FDA website contains links to additional information about youth and tobacco, news and events, and resources for consumers, health professionals, and other groups.

Foundation for a Drug-Free World
1626 N. Wilcox Ave., Ste. 1297
Los Angeles, CA 90028
(888) NO-DRUGS (663-7848)
website: www.drugfreeworld.org

A nonprofit public benefit corporation, the Foundation for a Drug-Free World seeks to inform people about drugs to help them make knowledgeable decisions and live without drugs. The organization focuses on providing youth with facts and activities to deter them from ever beginning to use drugs. The foundation's website provides visitors with access to fact sheets on a range of commonly abused substances, including marijuana, alcohol, and prescription drugs. Interested individuals can also order or download free booklets about drugs.

National Center on Addiction and Substance Abuse at Columbia University (CASAColumbia)
633 Third Ave., 19th Fl.
New York, NY 10017-6706
(212) 841-5200
website: www.casacolumbia.org

CASAColumbia works to produce quality research that examines the ways in which substance abuse influences American society and citizens and to utilize this research to formulate improved policy and practices. The two main divisions of the organization are Health and Treatment Research and Analysis, and Policy Research and Analysis. The CASAColumbia website provides a collection of downloadable reports, including "National Survey of American Attitudes on Substance Abuse

XVII: Teens" and "Addiction Medicine: Closing the Gap Between Science and Practice."

National Council on Problem Gambling (NCPG)
730 Eleventh St. NW, Ste. 601
Washington, DC 20001
(202) 547-9204
fax (202) 547-9206
e-mail: ncpg@ncpgambling.org
website: www.ncpgambling.org

The NCPG provides a national voice for problem gamblers and their families by advocating on their behalf at the local, state, and national levels. The council works to raise awareness about the problems associated with pathological gambling, to increase the number of treatment options for problem gamblers and their families, and to promote prevention and education research and programs. The NCPG website provides extensive information about the definition of problem gambling along with public awareness information and details about where and how individuals can get treatment for their problem.

National Families in Action (NFIA)
PO Box 133136
Atlanta, GA 30333-3136
(404) 248-9676
e-mail: nfia@nationalfamilies.org
website: www.nationalfamilies.org

Since its founding in 1977, NFIA has worked to actively oppose the overturning of laws that make marijuana illegal, viewing its legalization as a dangerous addition to the already legal alcohol and tobacco industries. Over the years since its founding, and continuing today, NFIA has produced extensive research about drug abuse and the effects of drugs on the brain and body. As a part of its addiction studies program, the organization publishes science-based information about drug use along with definitions of drug-related terminology. This information and details about current NFIA campaigns can be found on the group's website.

National Institute on Drug Abuse (NIDA)
Office of Science Policy and Communications
Public Information and Liaison Branch

6001 Executive Blvd., Rm. 5213, MSC 9561,
Bethesda, MD 20892-9561
(301) 443-1124
e-mail: information@nida.nih.gov
website: www.drugabuse.gov

The NIDA is a branch of the National Institutes of Health and works to use science to understand and better address drug abuse and addiction within the United States. To achieve this goal, the institute conducts extensive research and then works to distribute the findings to the public to develop better methods of prevention and treatment and improve public policy on addiction and drug abuse. The NIDA website provides access to publications detailing the research findings, and NIDA for Teens (www.teens.drugabuse.gov) provides easily accessible information in the form of fact sheets, videos, and a blog.

Treatment Research Institute (TRI)
(215) 399-0980
fax (215) 399-0987
website: www.tresearch.org

The TRI has been working since 1982 to research, develop, and implement science-based modes of treatment for alcohol and drug abuse and addiction. Its research spans many areas, including behavioral treatments and applications, law and ethics, and adolescents. On the TRI website, each of these sections contains links to websites with additional information on the topic, as well as bibliographies of articles on these issues.

For Further Reading

Books

Dodes, Lance M. *The Heart of Addiction: A New Approach to Understanding and Managing Alcoholism and Other Addictive Behaviors.* New York: HarperCollins, 2002. A substance-abuse clinician argues that addiction is more than just a physical craving and examines common emotional factors that link addicts of all kinds. Through a rebuffing of certain myths about addiction and a sampling of success stories, he suggests ways to manage and overcome these compulsions.

Erickson, Carlton K. *The Science of Addiction: From Neurobiology to Treatment.* New York: Norton, 2007. This work focuses on the genetic and neurobiological components of addictive behavior. It also discusses recent treatments that are based on understanding addictions from this perspective.

Heyman, Gene M. *Addiction: A Disorder of Choice.* Cambridge, MA: Harvard University Press, 2009. Heyman contends that addiction is not a disease but a voluntary choice. He maintains that people tend to immoderately consume more of what they like, and, for some people, that can have negative consequences. Heyman also argues that recovery is a matter of personal responsibility overcoming poor behavior.

Hoffman, John, and Susan Froemke, eds. *Addiction: Why Can't They Just Stop?* New York: Rodale, 2007. A companion book to an HBO series, this work uses expert testimony and personal narrative to explore the social and individual costs of various chemical addictions. It argues that the devastating consequences of addiction cannot be arrested unless people move beyond blaming addicts to understanding the causes and treatments.

Kuhar, Michael. *The Addicted Brain: Why We Abuse Drugs, Alcohol, and Nicotine.* Upper Saddle River, NJ: FT, 2012. A neuroscientist uses brain modeling to explain why some people are more prone to addiction than others. He also offers what new treatments hold for combatting chemical addiction in the brain.

Kuhn, Cynthia, Scott Swartzwelder, and Wilkie Wilson. *Buzzed: The Straight Facts About the Most Used and Abused Drugs from Alcohol to Ecstasy.* 3rd ed. New York: Norton, 2008. Medical experts list twelve common categories of drugs and provide a detailed history of their use as well as a thorough explanation of how they work on the brain and the body. The second half of the volume discusses addiction in general and the ramifications of such behavior.

Lewis, Marc. *Memoirs of an Addicted Brain: A Neuroscientist Examines his Former Life on Drugs.* New York: PublicAffairs, 2012. A former drug abuser traces his destructive lifestyle and his eventual recovery to become a neuroscientist. He uses his professional training to examine his past life and the behavioral and physiological factors that led to his addictive lifestyle.

Nakken, Craig. *The Addictive Personality: Understanding the Addictive Process and Compulsive Behavior.* Center City, MN: Hazleden Foundation, 1996. Nakken, a lecturer and therapist, investigates the roots of addiction, citing genetic, social, and learned influences that promote compulsive behavior. He also traces the difficult path to recovery and stresses the importance of monitoring future behaviors.

Shavelson, Lonny. *Hooked: Five Addicts Challenge Our Misguided Drug Rehab System.* New York: New Press, 2002. The author follows five drug addicts in San Francisco as they try to get assistance from rehab programs to conquer their problems. The addicts relate their experiences with criminal courts, recovery programs, and residential facilities, revealing how the system often fails those in most need of help.

Sheff, Nic. *We All Fall Down: Living with Addiction.* New York: Hachette, 2012. A meth and heroin addict relates his tale of living through rehab clinics and relapses on his road to recovery. He emphasizes that recovery is not an end but a continual struggle with sobriety.

Periodicals

Arria, Amelia M., and A. Thomas McLellan. "Evolution of Concept, but Not Action, in Addiction Treatment," *Substance Use & Misuse*, June 2012.

Baird, Vanessa. "Legalize Drugs—All of Them!," *New Internationalist*, September 2012.

Barth, Amy. "The Switched-On Brain," *Discover*, September 2012.

Eban, Katherine, and Doris Burke. "Painful Medicine," *Fortune*, November 21, 2011.

Gengler, Amanda. "The Urge to Lose Money," *Money*, March 2007.

Giles, Jim. "The Immunity Fix," *New Scientist*, August 2, 2008.

Goldman, Bruce. "The Neuroscience of Need," *Stanford Medicine*, Spring 2012.

Grossman, Lev. "The Hyperconnected," *Time*, April 16, 2007.

Hartston, Heidi. "The Case for Compulsive Shopping as an Addiction," *Journal of Psychoactive Drugs*, January–March 2012.

Interlandi, Jeneen, and Raina Kelley. "What Addicts Need," *Newsweek*, March 3, 2008.

Karim, Reef, and Priya Chaudhri. "Behavioral Addictions: An Overview," *Journal of Psychoactive Drugs*, January–March 2012.

Kluger, Jeffrey. "The New Drug Crisis: Addiction by Prescription," *Time*, September 13, 2010.

Kosten, Thomas. "Shooting Down Addiction," *Scientist*, June 2011.

Kringelbach, Morten L., and Kent C. Berridge. "The Joyful Mind," *Scientific American*, August 2012.

Lawrence, Alison. "The Dope on Drug Sentencing," *State Legislatures*, December 2011.

Lee, Chris. "This Man Is Addicted to Sex," *Newsweek*, December 5, 2011.

Nation. "Breaking the Taboo," December 27, 2010.

Ritchie, Méabh. "Screen Burn," *Times Educational Supplement*, November 5, 2010.

Rosen, Christine. "The Confessional Culture," *Humanities*, January/February 2011.

Sheean, Liz. "Addiction: A Disorder of Choice an Interview with Gene Heyman," *Psychotherapy in Australia*, August 2011.

Specter, Michael. "Getting a Fix," *New Yorker*, October 17, 2011.

Verbeke, Emily M., and Karin Dittrick-Nathan. "Student Gambling," *Education Digest*, February 2008.

Wagner, Jennifer Seter. "When Play Turns to Trouble," *U.S. News & World Report*, May 19, 2008.

Wexler, Sarah Z., Lea Goldman, and Jihan Thompson, "The New Addictions," *Marie Claire*, March 2009.

Websites

Al-Anon Family Groups (www.al-anon.alateen.org). Al-Anon provides information on its 12-step alcohol recovery program as well as what people might expect from attending an Al-Anon meeting. The website has sections for teens, media, and treatment professionals. It houses podcasts from members telling of their experiences with the program, and it provides links to some program literature and *The Forum*, a magazine published by the organization.

Faces & Voices of Recovery (www.facesandvoicesofrecovery.org). Founded in 2001, this nonprofit organization seeks to give voice to recovering substance abuses in shaping public policy on drug control and other related issues. The organization's website offers links to its newsletter and stories of recovery from some of its members.

National Association for Children of Alcoholics (www.nacoa.org). This organization brings together professional research and personal commitment to reach out to children of parents coping with substance abuse. Its website holds information on drugs and their abuse, and it provides helpful program literature aimed at teachers and students.

National Institute on Drug Abuse (www.drugabuse.gov). This US government website details the science of drug abuse and addiction worldwide. It provides information on a host of abused substances and current treatment methods. It also offers research aimed at young people.

Substance Abuse and Mental Health Services Administration (www.samhsa.gov). This government organization is charged with improving the behavioral health of Americans and reducing the impact of substance abuse and mental illness on the nation's communities. The website provides data, charts, and publications (in English and Spanish) regarding drug abuse and treatment options in the United States.

Index

Picture Credits

© AP Images/Morry Gash, 29
© AP Images/Elaine Thompson, 79
© apply pictures/Alamy, 24
© Simon Belcher/Alamy, 14
© BSIP SA/Alamy, 49
© Gale/Cengage, 17, 25, 32, 44, 54, 66, 71, 80, 88, 100
© Henry Westheim Photography/Alamy, 74
© Frank Herholdt/Alamy, 53
© imagebroker/Alamy, 64
© jvphoto/Alamy, 99
© Photononstop/Alamy, 43
© Joe Raedle/Getty Images, 76
© Chris Rout/Alamy, 10, 37, 87
© Bridgette Sullivan/Outer Focus Photos/Alamy, 39